מסורה

ArtScroll Mesorah Series®

Rabbi Nosson Scherman / Rabbi Meir Zlotowitz

General Editors

Shema
Yisrael

THE THREE PORTIONS OF THE SHEMA
INCLUDING THE BEDTIME SHEMA / A NEW TRANSLATION
WITH A COMMENTARY ANTHOLOGIZED FROM
TALMUDIC, MIDRASHIC, AND RABBINIC SOURCES.

Published by

Mesorah Publications, ltd

סדר קריאת שמע
וקריאת שמע על המטה

Translation and commentary by
Rabbi Meir Zlotowitz

An Overview / "A Declaration of Faith," by
Rabbi Nosson Scherman

FIRST EDITION
Ten Impressions . . . February 1982 — September 2009

Published and Distributed by
MESORAH PUBLICATIONS, Ltd.
4401 Second Avenue
Brooklyn, New York 11232

Distributed in Europe by
LEHMANNS
Unit E, Viking Business Park
Rolling Mill Road
Jarrow, Tyne & Wear NE32 3DP
England

Distributed in Australia & New Zealand by
GOLDS WORLD OF JUDAICA
3-13 William Street
Balaclava, Melbourne 3183
Victoria Australia

Distributed in Israel by
SIFRIATI / A. GITLER — BOOKS
6 Hayarkon Street
Bnei Brak 51127

Distributed in South Africa by
KOLLEL BOOKSHOP
Ivy Common 105 William Road
Norwood 2192, Johannesburg, South Africa

ARTSCROLL MESORAH SERIES ®
SHEMA YISRAEL / THE THREE PORTIONS OF THE SHEMA
© Copyright 1982, 2009, by MESORAH PUBLICATIONS, Ltd.
4401 Second Avenue / Brooklyn, N.Y. 11232 / (718) 921-9000 / www.artscroll.com

---

ISBN 10: 0-89906-187-7 / ISBN 13: 978-0-89906-187-0

Typography by Compuscribe at ArtScroll Studios, Ltd.
4401 Second Avenue / Brooklyn, N.Y. 11232 / (718) 921-9000

Printed in the United States of America
Bound by Sefercraft, Quality Bookbinders, Ltd. Brooklyn, N.Y.

An Overview /
A Declaration of Faith

אָמַר לָהֶם הקב״ה לְיִשְׂרָאֵל, אַתֶּם עֲשִׂיתוּנִי חֲטִיבָה
אַחַת בָּעוֹלָם שֶׁנֶּאֱמַר שְׁמַע יִשְׂרָאֵל ה׳ אֱלֹהֵינוּ ה׳
אֶחָד; וַאֲנִי אֶעֱשֶׂה אֶתְכֶם חֲטִיבָה אַחַת בָּעוֹלָם שֶׁנֶּאֱמַר
וּמִי כְּעַמְּךָ יִשְׂרָאֵל גּוֹי אֶחָד בָּאָרֶץ.

*The Holy One, Blessed is He, said to Israel,
You have declared Me unique in the universe,
as it says (Deuteronomy 6:4), Hear O Israel,
HASHEM, is [now] our God, HASHEM [will be]
One* — and I shall declare you unique in the
universe as it says (I Chronicles 17:21): And
who is like Your people Israel — a unique
nation on earth (Berachos 6a).*

Morning and night, the Jew shuts his eyes and
proclaims the *Shema* — God is ours and He is One.
Life's most Life's most meaningful moments are punctuated with the
meaningful *Shema*: when the Jew prepares to read the Torah on
moments are Sabbaths and festivals, when he dedicates his new day
punctuated with the and when he surrenders to helpless sleep in the unknown
Shema. night, at the climax of Yom Kippur, and at the climax of
life when his soul leaves its earthly host. In the *mezuzah*
the *Shema* sanctifies his home and in his *tefillin* it
sanctifies his intellect and strength. And God Himself
thanks Israel, as it were, for declaring His uniqueness by
means of the *Shema*, as though *He* becomes fulfilled
through *us*. Let us explore, in an elementary way, the
significance of the *Shema*; if we succeed we shall be both
better servants of God and better people.

I. R' Akiva's Example

Source One of the Talmud's most moving narratives tells of
of Life Rabbi Akiva's last days. He lived in the century after
the destruction of the Second Temple, a time when
Roman cruelty had brought Jewish life to one of its

---

* The unfamiliar translation of the first verse of *Shema* follows *Rashi's* commentary to the Torah. He explains: although at present only Israel recognizes HASHEM as God, in time to come He will be acknowledged by all mankind. See commentary p. 15.

lowest ebbs ever. The Romans sought to eradicate Judaism as an independent culture, and their primary target was Torah education. To ordain rabbis and to teach Torah publicly were declared criminal offenses punishable by death. R' Akiva would not knuckle under. He was the teacher of thousands, the nation's greatest sage, and one of its most devoted leaders. He knew that he was one of Rome's prime targets, but at a time when Israel's faith was under assault [שְׁעַת הַשְׁמָד], personal safety, even survival, cannot take priority to the survival of Torah and the needs of the people. If R' Akiva were to withhold his teaching and his personal example, he would become the passive ally of the Roman executioners.

If R' Akiva were to withhold his teaching and his personal example, he would become the passive ally of the Roman executioners.

R' Akiva knew what he had to do. He gathered large congregations publicly and taught them Torah.

His friend and colleague, Papus ben Yehudah, was appalled at R' Akiva's temerity.

Akiva, aren't you afraid of the government?'

R' Akiva answered, 'I will explain our predicament with a parable. Once a fox was walking along a river bank when he saw schools of fish frenziedly swimming from one part of the river to another. He called out to the fish, "From what do you flee?"

'The fish answered, "We seek to escape the nets that fishermen put out to catch us."

'Feigning concern, the fox shouted, "If only you would come up on the dry land! Then you and I could live together as peaceful neighbors, just as our forebears did before humans came along to disturb our harmony."

'The fish responded, "Are you the fox, about whom it is said that you are the shrewdest of all animals? You are not shrewd, but a fool! If our lives are in danger even in the water which is our source of life, how much greater would be our peril on land where our death is certain?"

'We are in the same predicament,' R' Akiva told Papus. 'If we are in danger when we study the Torah, about which we are taught *for it is your life and the length of your days (Deuteronomy 30:20)*, then our very survival will surely be in danger if we forsake the Torah!'

'If we are in danger when we study the Torah, then our very survival will surely be in danger if we forsake the Torah!'

Before long, Roman soldiers discovered R' Akiva and threw him into a dungeon — and not long afterward Papus ben Yehudah, too, was arrested and imprisoned together with him. Upon seeing his dear friend, Papus exclaimed, 'Akiva, how fortunate you are — *you* were

arrested for the sake of Torah. But sad it is for Papus — I was arrested for a mere triviality.'

It was the time of the morning *Shema* reading when R' Akiva was taken out to be tortured to death publicly. The Romans tore his flesh with iron combs, but during his frightful ordeal he accepted God's sovereignty upon himself by reciting the *Shema*. He was joyous, oblivious to the pain. Turnus Rufus, the Roman commander who ordered the barbarous execution, was flabbergasted. 'Have you no feeling of pain that you can laugh in the face of such intense suffering!' he exclaimed. Even R' Akiva's own students wondered, 'Our teacher, even to this extent?'

The dying sage explained, 'All my life I was concerned over a phrase of the Torah. We are taught in the *Shema* to accept God's sovereignty and decrees upon ourselves בְּכָל נַפְשְׁךָ, *with all your soul* — even if He takes your life.

I used to wonder if I would ever have the privilege of serving God to such a degree. Now that the chance has come to me, shall I not grasp it with joy?'

I used to wonder if I would ever have the privilege of serving God to such a degree. Now that the chance has come to me, shall I not grasp it with joy?'

He repeated the first verse of *Shema* — *Hear O Israel, HASHEM is [now] our God, HASHEM [will be] One* — and he drew out the word אֶחָד, *One,* until his soul left him.

A Heavenly voice was heard, saying, 'You are praiseworthy, R' Akiva, for your soul left you as you proclaimed God's Oneness! ... You are praiseworthy, R' Akiva, for you are ready to enter the life of the World to Come' *(Berachos* 61b; *Yerushalmi Berachos* 9:5).

R' Akiva remains one of the most inspirational figures in the last two thousand years. At the age of forty, he was still an ignorant, scholar-hating shepherd, when, thanks to the prodding and encouragement of an equally inspirational wife, he began learning how to read. Many years later he returned home surrounded by twenty-four thousand students and acclaimed as his people's leading scholar, but he accorded public honor to his poverty-stricken wife, telling his students, 'Whatever I have attained and whatever your have attained is due to her.' He became a leader of the military and spiritual resistance to Rome and, through his students, he became the dominant Torah figure of his turbulent, tormented era and the following generations.

He summed up his entire life in a final act of heroism: he placed the survival of Israel as a Torah nation ahead of personal safety.

But at the end, he summed up his entire life in a final act of heroism: he placed the survival of Israel as a Torah nation ahead of personal safety; and he taught one of his

greatest lessons as his soul expired. It is a worthy life's goal — even for a life as rich as R' Akiva's — to end on a note of total dedication to God. All his life he had declared his willingness to submerge his individuality to the goal of sanctifying God's Name, but no man can know if he will be equal to the awful challenge when it comes. R' Akiva's rejoicing eclipsed his suffering because he had proven equal to the ideals he taught. Turnus Rufus, his executioner, thought he was mad, but who remembers Turnus Rufus today? He thought he was wiping R' Akiva off the ledger of history, but Turnus Rufus is remembered only because of his notorious act, while his victim's memory lives on as one of the greatest people of the last two thousand years.

Turnus Rufus, his executioner, thought he was mad, but who remembers Turnus Rufus today?

The Prerequisite

Judaism has no special commandments for its Abrahams, Davids, and Akivas. If R' Akiva took comfort from his suffering in having declared the Oneness of God, if he considered his life a success because he was able to end it with a declaration that ה' אֶחָד, *HASHEM is One* — and if the Talmud and the Heavenly voice put so much stress upon it — then we must draw the lesson that the attainment of such a conviction is the duty of every man, woman, and child. Indeed, the twice-daily reading of the *Shema* is not only commanded by the Torah, it is the basic expression of Jewish belief.

When God gave Israel the Ten Commandments at Sinai, all Israel heard the first two directly from Him. The first commandment was God's declaration that He is God: *I am HASHEM your God ...*, the second commandment was the precept against belief in any other deity: *You shall not recognize the gods of others before My presence.* These are the cardinal commandments of Judaism, that we believe absolutely in God's existence and that we not share His mantle with any other being or power. As the Sages put it, only after a king's subjects acknowledge his legitimate authority can he promulgate decrees. Unless a government is recognized, it has no legal standing and its laws have no force. The first commandment, therefore, must be to believe in God, for without that prerequisite nothing else in the Torah could be binding. The second commandment is, in effect, a corollary of the first, that Divinity has no partners; there is one God and none other.

The first commandment, therefore, must be to believe in God, for without that prerequisite nothing else in the Torah could be binding.

The reading of *Shema* is our daily fulfillment of the

first commandment: that we declare our firm belief in God's existence and indivisibility *(Ramban* and *R' Bachya* to *Deut.* 6:4; but cf. *Rambam, Sefer HaMitzvos, Aseh* 1,2; and *Ramban* to *Lo Sa'aseh* 5).

Why does the profession of our faith require a declaration of God's Oneness? Why did R' Akiva draw out the word אֶחָד, *One,* until his death? — obviously this aspect of his final moments was critical, for it was followed by a Heavenly voice praising him for giving up his soul as he proclaimed that God is One, and announcing that he was entering the World to Come.

II. Oneness — The Ultimate Goal

Uniqueness and Control There are two aspects of God's Oneness: a) Nothing else is comparable to Him; b) nothing exists independently of Him.

When we say that God is One, we mean not only that there is none other, but that He is beyond comparison. *Rambam's* second Principle of Faith states:

> *I believe with perfect faith that the Creator, Blessed is His Name, is unique, and no uniqueness resembles His in any manner ...*

There is only one Mount Everest, but there are other mountains, though not so high. The Pacific is the largest ocean, but there are others. Moses was the greatest prophet and Solomon was the wisest man, and Scripture assures us that no one would ever equal them. Nevertheless, there have been many prophets and scholars of rare genius. Consequently any manifestation of physical, cultural, or intellectual greatness can be called 'unique' only in relative terms — it is great, greater, or greatest, but others, though inferior, can be compared to it. Not so God's uniqueness. He has no beginning or end, no limitations, no competitors or partners, no corporeality. We cannot comprehend any aspect of His existence because our conception and even our vocabulary is limited by our very humanness. Our ears cannot hear even most of the soundwaves audible to a dog, our vision is limited to what our most powerful telescopes can show us, and all the power of modern science cannot quell a hurricane or light up the night. An atomic explosion gives as much light as the sun for the barest instant and over a limited space, but the sun

We cannot comprehend any aspect of His existence because even our vocabulary is limited by our very humanness.

illuminates half a planet without stop, and our sun is smaller than millions of others in the solar system. Yet all the suns combined are but a small part of the universe and God created them all! When we think of such uniqueness, the very word 'unique' seems ludicrously inadequate to describe it.

When we think of such uniqueness, the very word 'unique' seems ludicrously inadequate to describe it.

The second aspect of God's Oneness is that God is the source of everything we know. Not only did He create the universe and endow its various components with the powers and instincts to function, reproduce, and be creative, He retains ultimate control over them. Even their apparent power extends only within the limits He places upon them. But this concept goes much deeper. God has a plan for the universe and every event somehow fits into this plan. There are variations, of course, because man has freedom of choice. Most of the time, we do not understand how the parts relate to the whole; often events seem so evil or incomprehensible that we cannot imagine how a merciful, rational Creator could have included them in His program. But even these apparent aberrations fit into the master plan. Sometimes, hindsight offers us a vantage point of a grand design.

He is King

If God rules everything and God, by definition, is all good, how can there be evil and sinners? Evil is a product of ignorance — ignorance of His Will and the concealment of His Presence. People don't stumble at high noon; they trip when night conceals the obstacles in their path, or when greed and passion persuade them to close their eyes. This is why 'night' and 'darkness' have become synonyms for suffering and evil and why it is said, in the words of *Tzeidah LaDerech,* מְעַט מִן הָאוֹר דּוֹחֶה הַרְבֵּה מִן הַחֹשֶׁךְ, *A little bit of light banishes much darkness.* Obviously if people were not blind to the truth, the achievement of God's goal would come much more quickly. That people do not see Him and are seduced by evil does not defeat His plan, however. One way or another, every epoch and event has its place. A nation can play a constructive role by being a force for good, but if it chooses to do otherwise, its eventual punishment and downfall can serve as a lesson that God's will cannot be flouted with impunity. In the longed-for time when God provides us with a true perspective on history will we will know how sinners failed, and that knowledge will sanctify His Name — clearly the sinful person or

Obviously if people were not blind to the truth, the achievement of God's goal would come much more quickly.

community would have played its part better had it sanctified Him in a more positive way, but the fullfillment of His will is inevitable, for all of creation exists only for that purpose. This is the ultimate dimension of God's Oneness: it means that everything is inseparable from His control and guidance.

Sometimes mankind basks in the light of His mercy and the human mind is illuminated by the brilliance of comprehending Him. Other times we shudder in the chill of night and our perceptions are clouded by our failure to understand His ways. These are the spiritual days and nights of our existence. In either kind of experience we must find ways to strengthen our faith in Him as our God, our Creator, our all-powerful Guide; and we must proclaim our conviction that He is One and that any other claimants to power are impostors.

God's essence does not become enhanced by our acknowledgment of Him. God's essence does not become enhanced by our acknowledgment of Him; the Name אֱלֹהִים, *God,* describes Him as the Ultimate Power, and as such He becomes no stronger by virtue of our recognition or weaker by virtue of our denial. But God wants something more. In His wisdom He decreed that His creatures should declare Him to be King. In Jewish thought, there is a difference between a מֹשֵׁל, *dictator,* and a מֶלֶךְ, *king.* The despot is not dependent on the good will of his subjects; he imposes his will whether or not it is welcome. But the 'King' acquires that title in its most meaningful sense only with the respect and consent of the governed. If his subjects accept his legitimacy he earns the Hebrew title מֶלֶךְ, *king,* otherwise, no matter how absolute his power, he is called a מֹשֵׁל, *dictator.* [This concept is discussed at length in the Overview to *Vayigash.*] God

God wants to be more than our Master; He wants to be our King and for this to happen we must accept His reign. wants to be more than our Master; He wants to be our King and for this to happen we must accept His reign.

All of this we accomplish when we recite the *Shema.* We proclaim our faith. We declare our knowledge — though our understanding may be far from perfect — that His will is done through every event, from the holy to the heinous. We accept God as our King — willingly, gladly, with a sense of privilege that He lowers Himself to let us serve Him; indeed, that He lets us be necessary to the accomplishment of His goals. Night and day we recite the *Shema,* symbolizing our acceptance of these ideals in every period and every condition of life. In the golden era of David and Solomon or on the racks of Torquemada's

Inquisition and under the swords of the Crusaders, Israel declares its faith and finds comfort in the knowledge that HASHEM is *our* God — for He revealed Himself to us and relies upon us to pierce the darkness of human perception with the light of His Oneness.

R' Akiva's How easy it is to declare that God is King, Creator, and
Triumph Guide of *others* — and how hard it is to accept His sovereignty over our*selves*. How easy to tell others that *their* travail is justified and that *they* must subject their urges and resources to His will — and how hard to admit that it was not a miscarriage of justice that we stubbed *our* toe or failed to gain riches and respect. How easy to preach that Israel in general has a demanding responsibility as the recipient of God's Torah and the bearer of his mission — but how hard for each son and daughter of Israel to live *his* own life, *her* own life, in accordance with that awareness.

R Akiva personified everything that is sublime in Israel. From ignoramus he made himself the teacher of Israel. In times of the most intense national chagrin and degradation, he inspired others to confidence and
God as King hardly optimism. God as King hardly had a subject who served
had a subject who Him better. But R' Akiva's own heroic demonstration of
served Him better. Israel's courage in God's service left him the helpless prey of Turnus Rufus' torturers!

Dismay? No, R' Akiva was not dismayed. All his life he had prepared himself for the moment when even his life would be offered upon the altar of his King — the God whom *he* had made King. In the face of the blaspheming Turnus Rufus and in the presence of his grieving but inspired students, he taught his last and greatest lesson. Everything in life is God's gift and every event is a piece in the construction of His jigsaw puzzle. If R' Akiva's contribution had to be through the
A heavenly voice endurance of pain with the ecstatic conviction that even
testified to his good his suffering had meaning, then so be it.
fortune as the gates In his dying moments he proclaimed the *Shema* — and
of the World to a heavenly voice testified to his good fortune as the gates
Come swung open of the World to Come swung open to admit R' Akiva.
to admit R' Akiva.

Rabbi Nosson Scherman
Shevat 6, 5742

סדר קריאת שמע

◀§ Some essential laws pertaining to the recital of the Shema

The following has been culled from *Shulchan Aruch* and *Likkutei Mahariach*. Other laws have been inserted in their appropriate places in the commentary and as instructions within the Text.

☐ Before beginning the *Shema* one must bear in mind that he intends to fulfill the commandment of reciting the *Shema* twice daily.

☐ The first verse of *Shema* is the essential profession of our faith. It should be recited aloud in order to arouse one's full concentration on its meaning and significance.

☐ Some consider it preferable to recite the entire *Shema* aloud (except for the passage בָּרוּךְ שֵׁם) in order to arouse the concentration. However, at the minimum, the first verse should be said aloud, while the rest of *Shema* may be recited quietly, provided one hears what he is saying.

☐ Every word of the *Shema* must be recited with *kavannah* — concentration upon its meaning. All thoughts other than God's Unity must be shut out while the *Shema* is recited with concentration of heart and mind.

☐ While reciting the first verse, it is customary to cover the eyes with the right hand to avoid distraction and enhance the concentration.

☐ Although it is not the universal custom to chant the *Shema* with the cantillation melody used during the Synagogue Torah reading, it is laudable to do so unless one finds that such chanting interferes with his concentration. In any event, the punctuation must be followed so that phrases are grouped together properly in accordance with the syntax of each word-group and verse.

☐ Every word must be enunciated clearly and uttered with the correct grammatical emphasis. It is especially important to enunciate clearly and pause briefly between words ending and beginning with the same consonant, such as בְּכָל לְבָבְכֶם, וַאֲבַדְתֶּם מְהֵרָה, to avoid slurring, and between words one of which ends with a consonant and one of which begins with a silent letter [א or ע], such as אֲשֶׁר אָנֹכִי, הַיּוֹם עַל אֶתְכֶם, וּרְאִיתֶם אֹתוֹ.

☐ The last word of the first verse, אֶחָד, must be pronounced with special emphasis [see commentary], while one meditates on God's sovereignty over the seven heavens and earth, and the four directions — east, south, west, and north.

☐ While reciting the three portions of the *Shema*, one may not communicate with someone else by winking or motioning with the lips or fingers.

☐ During morning services, the four *tzitzis* are to be gathered when one says the words וַהֲבִיאֵנוּ לְשָׁלוֹם, *Bring us in peace*, in the paragraph preceding the *Shema* in the siddur. From then on and throughout the *Shema*, the *tzitzis* are to be held — according to some customs, between the fourth finger and the little finger — against the heart.

☐ When reciting the third portion, וַיֹּאמֶר ה', *HASHEM said*, during morning services, one should also grasp the *tzitzis* with the right hand and look at them, until after he has said the words לְנֶאֱמָנִים וְנֶחְמָדִים לָעַד in the אֱמֶת וְיַצִּיב prayer following *Shema*.

Immediately before reciting the *Shema* one must concentrate on his intention to fulfill the positive commandment of reciting the *Shema* twice daily.

When praying in private or without a minyan, add the following three-word formula

אֵל מֶלֶךְ נֶאֱמָן:

Before reciting the following verse, concentrate upon accepting God's absolute sovereignty. Then recite it aloud:

שְׁמַע יִשְׂרָאֵל יהוה אֱלֹהֵינוּ יהוה | אֶחָד:

After a short pause, the following verse is said in a whisper
[except on Yom Kippur when it is recited aloud]:

בָּרוּךְ שֵׁם כְּבוֹד מַלְכוּתוֹ לְעוֹלָם וָעֶד.

◂§ The Shema/Preliminary Formula:

אֵל מֶלֶךְ נֶאֱמָן — *God, trustworthy King.* These three words are not part of the Biblical verses; they are added as an introductory formula in the liturgy when one recites *Shema* in the absence of a *minyan.* [When praying with a minyan this three-word formula is not recited; instead one listens to the *chazzan's* three-word repetition of the conclusion ה' אֱלֹהֵיכֶם אֱמֶת (see *comm.* below, p. 47).]

The reason for adding three words — at the beginning or the end — is as follows: The three paragraphs of the *Shema* contain a total of 245 words. The additional three words yield the total number of both the positive commandments and the organs in the human body. This expresses the concept that physical existence is indivisible from the spiritual obligation to obey the precepts of the Torah in their entirety.

The Sages accordingly maintain that "whoever recites the *Shema* with its 248 words in proper concentration will merit that the Holy One, Blessed be He, will watch over his every organ. — 'Watch over

Mine,' said God, 'and I will watch over yours' " (*Midrash Tanchuma*; see *Daas Zekeinim*).

These words — the initials of which spell אָמֵן (*Shabbos* 19b) — were chosen to supply the three words needed for the total of 248 because they succinctly express the essence of our belief in God.

The *kavannah* [concentration of thought on the meaning of the words] one should have while reciting the formula is:

□ אֵל, *God* — You exist as the All-Powerful source of all mercy;

□ מֶלֶךְ, *King* — You rule, lead, and exercise supervision over all;

□ נֶאֱמָן, *trustworthy* — In dispensing reward and punishment, You are fair and scrupulous, apportioning no more suffering nor less good than one deserves (*Etz Yosef*).

According to *Rokeach* the *kavannah* is upon the initials אָמֵן, and upon the intimation of the words: אֵל, *God* — before Creation; מֶלֶךְ, *king* — over all of this world; נֶאֱמָן, *trustworthy* — to resurrect the dead at the time of Redemption.

◂§ The First Portion [*Deut.* 6:4-9]

In its Scriptural context: The first portion of *Shema* is in *Parshas Va'eschanan, Deuteronomy* 6:4-9. It was enunciated by Moses to the Israelites after he recounted the story of the Giving of the Ten Commandments, in the general context of Moses' eloquent appeal that the Jewish nation not forget what they had personally witnessed at the Revelation, and that they obey God's laws. Then he proceeded to declare the other foundation of the Torah: the Oneness of God and Israel's undivided love and loyalty to Him.

According to *Yerushalmi Berachos* 1:5 these following sections were chosen to form the daily reading of the *Shema* because their verses contain parallel allusions to the Ten Commandments. [See p. 63.]

Rambam notes that this passage is closely tied to the First Commandment — *I am HASHEM your God* — inasmuch as that commandment contains the principal of the unity

Immediately before reciting the *Shema* one must concentrate on his intention
to fulfill the positive commandment of reciting the *Shema* twice daily.

When praying in private or without a minyan, add the following three-word formula

God, Trustworthy King.

Before reciting the following verse, concentrate upon accepting God's
absolute sovereignty. Then recite it aloud:

Deuteronomy
6:4
Hear, O Israel: HASHEM is [now] our God, HASHEM [will be] One.

After a short pause, the following verse is said in a whisper
[except on Yom Kippur when it is recited aloud]:

Pesachim
56a
Blessed be the Name of His glorious kingdom for all eternity.

of God. In the *Shema*, Moses intended to elaborate on that Commandment and he began
to do so soon after the Ten Commandments. This concept of God's absolute Unity is the
essence of our faith, and whoever does not acknowledge it, denies the primary principle of
our religion as if he worships idols.

◄§ **The First Verse/The** acceptance of
God's absolute sovereignty

The recitation of *Shema* — especially its
first verse — represents fulfillment of the
paramount commandment of עוֹל קַבָּלַת
מַלְכוּת שָׁמַיִם, *acceptance of God's absolute
sovereignty*. For by declaring that God is
One — Unique, and Indivisible — we
thereby sublimate every facet of our
personalities and possessions — our very
lives — to His will.

4. שְׁמַע יִשְׂרָאֵל ה' אֱלֹהֵינוּ ה' אֶחָד — *Hear, O
Israel: HASHEM is [now] our God,
HASHEM [will be] One* [literally, *HASHEM
is One; Alone; Unique*]. The translation
follows *Rashi*. The Sages and commentators find many layers of meaning in this
seminal verse — many of which will be
cited below in the word-by-word exposition — but the consensus is that *Rashi's*
interpretation is the minimum one must
have in mind when reciting the passage
since it takes into account every word,
allowing for no superfluity.

As *Rashi* explains it, the phrase means
"... *HASHEM*, Who now is only *our God*
and not that of other peoples [i.e., Who, in
this point in the history of the world is
acknowledged as the true God only by
Israel but not by all people of the earth] will
in the future be [acknowledged by *all* as]
the One [i.e., sole] *HASHEM.* Thus it is
written [*Zephaniah 3:9*]: ... *For then I will
turn to the peoples a pure language that
they may all call upon the Name of*

HASHEM; and it is further said [*Zechariah
14:9*]: *In that day* [of Ultimate Redemp-
tion] *shall HASHEM be One and His Name
One."*

That is, God's unity is absolute even
now, but the gentile nations do not
acknowledge Him as One; only Israel does.
In Messianic times, however, all the world
will acknowledge that He is the sole God.
Although the Sages derive the Biblical
concept of God's Unity from our passage,
if it enunciated only that — and did not
express the additional idea that what only
Israel acknowledges now will be acknowledged by all in the future — it would be
sufficient to have said: *Hear O Israel our
God is One*, or: *Hear O Israel: HASHEM is
One* (*Mizrachi; cf. Gur Aryeh; Tzeidah
LaDerech; Zikaron*).

Ibn Ezra explains the verse in *Zephaniah* cited
by *Rashi: For then I will turn to the peoples a
pure language*, i.e., the whole world will speak in
the Holy Tongue — Hebrew — *that they may all
call upon the Name of HASHEM ... In that day
HASHEM shall be One and his Name One.* That
is, God's Name will be One, for all will refer to
Him unanimously as *HASHEM* [i.e., the Four-
letter Name as it is written]. [See *Overview.*]

Among other interpretations of this
primary passage are:

□ R' Saadiah Gaon: *Know, Israel, that
HASHEM our God is the One God.*

□ Rashbam: ... *HASHEM alone is our
God and we have no other god with Him*
[comp. *II Chronicles 13:10*]; *HASHEM is
One* — Him only do we serve.

□ Ralbag: *Perceive well, O congregation of Israel:* He Who is referred to as 'HASHEM' oversees us; and though His Essence is beyond our meager comprehension, *HASHEM is One* — the Holy Being referred to by that Holy Name is One.

* * *

While reciting the *Shema*, one should concentrate on its parallels with the Ten Commandments [as listed on p. 63]. Since such prolonged concentration is difficult when one prays together with a congregation, at the very minimum one should concentrate on the first two Commandments alluded to in the first verse:

Hear O Israel, HASHEM is our God = I am HASHEM your God;

HASHEM is one = You shall not have any other gods.

These allusions are relatively easy to concentrate upon. It is known that these first two Commandments embrace all 613 *mitzvos*, since all of the positive commandments are implicit in *I am HASHEM your God*, while all the negative commandments are implicit in *You shall not have any other gods* (*Ba'er Hatev; Likkutei Mahariach*).

◆§ **Word-by-word exposition of the first verse:**

□ שְׁמַע — **Hear.** Not simply *listen*, but consider well; concentrate, understand and absorb (*Sforno; Ralbag*).

The term also connotes *acceptance* as distinguished from הָאֲזִן [from אֹזֶן, *ear*] which has the more literal connotation of inclining the ear to punctiliously listen [see *Rashi* to Exodus 15:26].

According to *Abudraham*, the term שְׁמַע implies testimony, as if each Israelite reciting the *Shema* tells his fellow: "Listen! I believe that HASHEM our God is the One and only God in the world." The letters ע and ד, which are written large in the Torah Scroll, form the word עֵד, *witness*. [See below: "The enlarged ע and ד."]

Abudraham also offers that the word שְׁמַע can be understood, homiletically, to form the initials of the steps by which one can learn to accept God's sovereignty: שְׂאוּ מָרוֹם עֵינֵיכֶם, *lift your eyes upward*, to realize that there is a purpose higher than your personal and physical needs and desires. When is the best time for this? שַׁחֲרִית מִנְחָה עַרְבִית, *at morning, afternoon, and evening prayers*. To whom? שַׁדַּי מֶלֶךְ עֶלְיוֹן, *to the Almighty, the exalted King*. If you do so, you will accept upon yourself

עוֹל מַלְכוּת שָׁמַיִם, *the yoke of the Heavenly kingdom*. [This last phrase begins with the letters of שְׁמַע although they are in reverse order.]

The Talmudic Sages derive several laws from the use in our verse of the word שְׁמַע, *hear*. A sampling:

The *Shema* may be recited in any language … for the Torah uses the expression *hear*, implying: בְּכָל לָשׁוֹן שֶׁאַתָּה שׁוֹמֵעַ, *In any language that you understand* [the verb שְׁמַע means both *hear* and *understand*] (*Berachos* 13a).

[The commentators explain that this applies only to one who does not understand Hebrew; one who understands Hebrew must read it in its original.]

Sefas Emes explains the connotation of the Talmudic dictum as follows: In every message that your ears absorb, *hear* in them: HASHEM our God is the One God. In everything perceive His greatness and Oneness; everything attests to Him.

R' Yose in the Talmud perceives a more literal connotation to *hear*: He who recites the *Shema* must do so audibly so he hears what he is reciting, for it says שְׁמַע, *hear*, which implies let your ear hear what you recite with your mouth (*Berachos* 15a).

That is, mental concentration on the *Shema* is not sufficient to fulfill the primary obligation [לְכַתְּחִלָּה]. If בְּדִיעֲבָד, *de facto*, one had recited the *Shema* inaudibly he has fulfilled his duty, but he must not do so regularly. [See also *v.* 6 below עַל לְבָבֶךָ, and *v.* 7 s.v. וְדִבַּרְתָּ בָּם.]

One who recites the *Shema* must direct his concentration on it since it says here שְׁמַע יִשְׂרָאֵל, *Hear O Israel*, and in another passage [*Deut.* 27:9] הַסְכֵּת וּשְׁמַע יִשְׂרָאֵל, *pay attention and hear, O Israel*. The similar expression shows that just as the latter 'hearing' must be accompanied by attention, so here it must be accompanied by attention (*Berachos* 16a).

□ יִשְׂרָאֵל — **Israel.** The term *Israel* — technically the spiritual name of the Patriarch Jacob [see *Gen.* 32:29, and *ArtScroll* comm. to 49:1] — is a collective reference to the lofty role of the Jewish nation as a whole.

Since we now declare our acceptance of God's sovereignty and acknowledgment of His Oneness, every member of Israel must join in comprehending that message (*R' Nosson Scherman*).

There is a Midrashic view cited in the Talmud, however, that *Israel* in our passage refers personally to Jacob himself,

and that this passage, which the Torah now records in Moses' name, is a quotation of a statement of reassurance that Jacob's sons made to him on his deathbed before he granted them his final Patriarchal blessing. See footnote to בָּרוּךְ שֵׁם below.

□ ה' — HASHEM. The Divinity is known to us by several Names, each of which reflects another of His different Aspects or Attributes as it is perceived in His conduct with mankind (Sh'mos Rabbah 3:6).

◂§ The Shem HaMeforash

The Four-Letter Name י־ה־ו־ה used here is known as the *Shem HaMeforash*, 'the clarified Name' or 'the separated Name.' In respect for its great sanctity, nowadays it is never pronounced as it is written. The name *Adonoy* [my lord] is substituted for it in prayer, while in common speech it is reverently pronounced הַשֵּׁם, *HASHEM* ['The Name' *par excellence*], and is usually abbreviated in printed Hebrew as ה' or יְיָ.

God referred to Himself by this Four Letter Name in His revelation to Moses, as we can find in *Exodus* 3:15: '*HASHEM*' the God of your fathers ... זֶה שְׁמִי, this is My Name [לְעֹלָם] forever, and this is My memorial for all generations. As the Hebrew לְעֹלָם [forever] is spelled in the unvowelized Torah Scroll [לעלם instead of its usual spelling [לעולם], it could be read לְעַלֵּם [to conceal] — this is My name to be concealed. In this the Rabbis found an allusion to the rule that this Name may not be read as it is written: its pronunciation is to be concealed, but another word — *Adonay* — is to be reverently substituted for it [see *Rashi ad loc.; Kiddushin* 71a; *Sh'mos Rabbah* 3:9].

Only in the Temple did the *Kohen Gadol* [High Priest], while ministering in the Temple on Yom Kippur, and the *Kohanim* [Priests], when blessing the masses [בִּרְכַּת כֹּהֲנִים] daily in the Temple courtyard, pronounce the Name as it is written. On Yom Kippur, the High Priest recited the *Shem HaMeforash* in his recitation of *Levit.* 16:30 during the confession of sins. When the priests and the people in the great hall heard him utter the *Shem HaMeforash*, they would prostrate themselves and glorify God, saying: בָּרוּךְ שֵׁם כְּבוֹד מַלְכוּתוֹ לְעוֹלָם וָעֶד, *Blessed be the Name of His glorious Kingdom for all eternity (Mishnah Yoma* 6:27).

After the death of Shimon HaTzaddik, successor to Ezra and High Priest of the Second Temple Era, certain Divine manifestations were no longer evident in the Temple, and the *Shem HaMeforash* was no longer uttered by the Kohanim in their blessings [See *Yoma* 39a; *Sotah* 13:8; see also ArtScroll *Bircas Kohanim* p. 36].

Outside of the Temple, however, pronunciation of this Name was prohibited from earliest times [cf. *Mishnah Berachos* 9:5; *Sotah* 7:6; *Tamid* 7:2 and commentaries]. Among those who are excluded from a share in the World to Come is ''one who pronounces the Name according to its letters'' (*Mishnah Sanhedrin* 10:1).

◂§ Meanings of the Name HASHEM

The Name *HASHEM* is used to depict God in His aspect as Dispenser of Divine mercy [מִדַּת הָרַחֲמִים]. This is derived in *Sifre* [*Deut.* 3:24]: 'Wherever God is referred to as *HASHEM* it designates His Attribute of Mercy, as it is written [*Exodus* 34:6]: ה' ה' אֵל רַחוּם, *HASHEM, HASHEM, merciful God.*' It is the "personal" Name of the Divinity in His relationship with the Jews, and denotes His utter transcendence and that he is the Source of all existence and continuity [see *Kuzari* 2:2; *Moreh Nevuchim* 1:61].

The spelling of the Name י־ה־ו־ה, is interpreted to connote הָיָה, הֹוֶה, וְיִהְיֶה, literally *He was, He is, and He will be*; it denotes the level where past, present, and future are merged and all are the same *(Tur Orach Chaim* 5). That is, God is Eternal and all time is united within Him. He exists eternally and His essence is unchangeable.

According to R' Yonah in *Sefer HaYirah*, when mentioning HASHEM'S Name throughout *Shema*, no special concentration [*kavannah*] is required except that one must bear in mind the simple meaning of the Name as it is pronounced [*Adonay*], which denotes Supreme Master over all. Exceptions are the two times when "HASHEM" occurs in the first passage of *Shema*. In those cases one must prolong pronunciation of the Names and concentrate on their meaning as they are spelled as well, which is הָיָה הֹוֶה וְיִהְיֶה, *He was, is, and will be*, as explained above.

◂§ The Name "Elohim"

□ אֱלֹהֵינוּ — Our God. In contrast with *HASHEM*, אֱלֹהִים [*Elohim*] describes God in His *universal* aspect as Lord over all Creation. The word itself means All-Powerful — from אֵל, *power* — and is the Name used exclusively in the first chapter

of *Genesis*, the account of creation, since it denotes Him Who has the power to produce all things (see *Ikkarim* 1:11).

It appears in the plural form [with the suffix יִם] "as a matter of reverence, for every language has its reverent form of address [as in 'the plural of majesty'], but no idea of Divine plurality is to be inferred from this form, as evidenced by the fact that the verbs associated with it — for example בָּרָא, *created*, in *Gen.* 1:1 — are in singular" (*Ibn Ezra, Gen.* 1:1).

In essence, this Name depicts God in His aspect as Dispenser of Justice [מִדַּת הַדִּין] — Ruler, Director, Law-giver, and Judge of the World. [The latter translation is derived in *Sifre* to *Deut.* 3:24 (see above "*Meanings of the Name*," which continues): "Wherever God is referred to as *Elohim* it designates His Attribute of Justice."]

Rambam notes that in other passages where Moses' speech to Israel is recorded, Moses normally used the second person and would say 'your God,' as for example [*Deut.* 9:1-3]: '*Hear, O Israel, you are about to pass over the Jordan this day ... know, therefore, that HASHEM your God goes with you*'; and even in our very next verse: '*And You shall love HASHEM your God.*' In our passage, which is a declaration of God's unity, however, Moses changed his normal usage and said '*our God*' [thus including himself in this profession of our faith, for had he used the second person he might have appeared to have been excluding himself from this declaration *(R' Bachya; Racanati; Ma'or VaShemesh)*].

Haamek Davar cites *Rambam* and adds that, following the Midrashic tradition, another reason Moses used the second person was to cite *verbatim* the ancient formula ascribed to Jacob's sons, to give it [at God's command] the full force of Torah. "Similarly, there are many passages in Scripture that were well known before that particular prophet, who, under the guidance of the Prophetic Spirit, inscribed them in his book. In any event, the first two sections of *Shema* were already known in Israel before the people came to the plains of Moab [where Moses recorded them], for the people were already obligated in the *mitzvah* of *tefillin*" [which included these two sections].

⋘ Meanings of the Name "Elohim"

The primary explanation of *Elohim* are:

• A Name that, throughout Scriptures, signifies מָרוּת, *authority* (*Rashi* on *Deut.* 6:2);

• It denotes God as 'chief' *(Rambam)*;

• It is a term signifying 'Proprietor' or 'Governor' of the world in broad terms; or in narrower terms, it designates a human judge (see *Kuzari* 4);

• It denotes God as the Eternal and Everlasting. Human judges are referred to as *Elohim* (in *Exodus* 22:8) because they judge 'in the image of God' *(Sforno)*;

• It describes God as 'the Mighty One who wields authority over the beings Above and Below' *(Tur Orach Chaim* 5);

• It describes God as בַּעַל הַיְכוֹלָת, *the Omnipotent*, the All-Powerful (*Shulchan Aruch* ibid.);

• In the plural form it signifies the many forces that are spread throughout Creation. All these forces emanate from the One God, and in Him are found the sources of all forces in complete unity *(Malbim)*;

• It indicates the sum total of His attributes and powers united in Him (see *Overview*).

□ ה' אֶחָד — **HASHEM the One.** He is One in two essential senses: a) because there is no other God but He; b) because He is totally Unique in all existence, and hence beyond all comparison with anything else (*Akeidah; Rashbam*).

Though we perceive God in many roles — kind, angry, merciful, wise, judging, and so on — these are not different moods or attitudes as they would be in the multifaceted personality of a human being. Rather, all flow from a unified purpose and existence which is beyond our comprehension, but which we tend to understand only in terms of our limited perceptions.

Harav Gedaliah Schorr likened this concept to a ray of light seen through a prism. Though it is seen as a myriad of different colors, it is a single ray of light. So, too, God's many manifestations are truly one.

The entire concept that God is incorporeal — i.e., that He is Spirit and not matter — finds its root in our passage, which establishes this Divine unity. As *Rambam* writes in *Moreh Nevuchim* 2:1; "Nothing corporeal can be a unity, either because everything corporeal is divisible or because it is compound; that is to say, logically it can be separated into elements. Because something can be identified as a distinct and particular body only when a distinguishing

element is added to its corporeal elemental substratum, it must include at least two elements. But it has been proven that the Absolute allows for no dualism whatever."

When saying the word אֶחָד, One, a person should draw out the second syllable a bit and emphasize the final consonant. The first syllable, אֶ, is not to be drawn out. While saying the א, which has the numerical value of one, one should think of the unity of God. While drawing out the ח (a letter with the numerical value of eight), one should bear in mind that God is Master of the earth and the seven heavens. While clearly enunciating the final ד (which has the numerical value of four), one should bear in mind that God is Master in all four directions, meaning everywhere (Berachos 13b; Rokeach; Semak; see Shulchan Aruch).

The Sages note that "whoever prolongs the word אֶחָד has his days and years prolonged" because he prolongs the word in order to concentrate more intensively on God's mastery over all aspects of existence (Berachos ibid.).

According to the Talmudic and Midrashic interpretation which attributes this verse to Jacob's children, this phrase implies: "We are united in our common belief in God — Just as there is only One [God] in your heart, so in our heart there is only One". [See comm. to בָּרוּךְ שֵׁם.]

◈§ The enlarged ע and ד

In Torah scrolls, the letters ע of שְׁמַע and ד of אֶחָד are written large. Together they form the word עֵד, witness. As the commentators explain, the inner implication of the enlarged letters is to allude to the thought that every Israelite, by pronouncing the Shema, becomes one of HASHEM'S witnesses, declaring His Unity to all the world (Abudraham; Kol Bo; Rokeach).

Sforno perceives that the enlarged ד, with the numerical value of four, draws attention to God's uniqueness. There are three lower forms of existence: that of earth with animal and vegetable life that are both subject to death and decomposition; that of the heavenly spheres; and that of the spiritual beings like angels. God is a 'fourth' form of existence, he is incomparably elevated and removed from any of the others. The enlarged ע [ayin means 'eye'] of שְׁמַע suggests that it is proper to open wide our eye and concentrate on these great and sublime matters.

Kabbalistically, the enlarged ד alludes to the additional verse — Blessed be the Name of His glorious kingdom for all eternity — that is added to the daily recital of the Shema, but which was not recorded in the Torah (Rambam; R' Bachya).

According to R' Hirsch, following Baal HaTurim, the practical reason for the enlarged ד is to distinguish אֶחָד 'ה, One God, from the blasphemous reading 'חִ אַחֵר, another God. Conversely, we find that in Exodus 34:14 — You shall not bow לְאֵל אַחֵר, to another god — the ר in אַחֵר is written large, in order that one should not utter erroneously the blasphemy: You shall not bow לְאֵל אֶחָד, to One God. The ע in Shema is also enlarged, possibly to avoid an interchange with the letter א which would yield in the blasphemous reading: שְׁמָא יִשְׂרָאֵל, perhaps, O Israel. Together, the enlarged letters ע and ד, form the word עֵד, meaning testimony or witness. This expresses that whoever recites Shema Yisrael appoints himself as a witness to himself and to the world testifying to God's unity.

◈§ The response of Jacob and the angels

בָּרוּךְ שֵׁם כְּבוֹד מַלְכוּתוֹ לְעוֹלָם וָעֶד — Blessed be the name of His glorious kingdom for all eternity [or: Blessed be the Name; His glorious kingdom is for all eternity]. Having proclaimed God as our King, we thank Him for granting us the privilege of serving Him, Whose kingdom is eternal and unbounded (Etz Yosef).

This verse is not included in the Torah, but is of very ancient origin. It was recited in the Temple as a response (similar to our Amen) whenever HASHEM'S Four-Letter Name was uttered in a blessing [Taanis 16b], and on Yom Kippur when the Kohen Gadol mentioned HASHEM'S Name on Yom Kippur in the Temple [Yoma 35a]. According to Bereishis Rabbah 865 it formed the angels' response to Israel's recital of the Shema [see below].

The Sages give two reasons for saying this verse silently:

(a) According to tradition, at Jacob's deathbed his children affirmed their loyalty to God by proclaiming the verse Shema. Jacob responded with the words Blessed be the Name, etc. The Sages taught: Should we say these words in our prayers because Jacob said it? Yes. But, on the other hand, Moses did not transmit it to us, for it is not found in the Torah. Therefore, let us say it

One should pause briefly before beginning the next paragraph so as to make a distinction between the primary acceptance of God's Heavenly Kingdom, and acceptance of the commandments, which is the theme of the following, a theme he should bear in mind before beginning the paragraph:

ה   וְאָהַבְתָּ אֵת יהוה אֱלֹהֶיךָ בְּכָל-לְבָבְךָ וּבְכָל-נַפְשְׁךָ

silently (Pesachim 56a).

(b) Moses heard this beautiful prayer from the angels, and taught it to Israel. We dare not say it aloud, because we are unworthy of using an angelic formula. On Yom Kippur, however, when Israel elevates itself to the sin-free level of angels, we may proclaim it loudly (Devarim Rabbah 2:36). [1]

◄§ Commandments of the first chapter: To love God; to think of the commandments; to instruct our children in the Torah; to recite God's word when retiring and arising; tefillin and mezuzah.

While reciting the first verse of this section, one should concentrate upon fulfilling the positive commandment to love HASHEM, which is one of the 248 positive commandments.

The first verse of Shema refers to God as He proclaims Himself to the entire nation; therefore the first verse describes Him in the plural as אֱלֹהֵינוּ, our God. The following section — worded in the singular — turns to each individual and portrays God to him as your personal God; this

emphasizes that each individual is the special object of God's love (R' Hirsch).

5. וְאָהַבְתָּ אֵת ה' אֱלֹהֶיךָ — (And) you shall love HASHEM your God. The meaning is: Fulfill His commandments out of love and not out of fear, for one who serves out of love is incomparably superior to one who serves out of fear. For in the case of one who serves his master out of fear, should the master trouble him excessively, he would leave him and go away (Rashi).

In another verse [Deut. 6:13), however, we read: HASHEM your God, you shall fear. We learn, accordingly, that we must conduct ourselves with the attributes of both fear and love: When we are tempted to indulge in something forbidden, fear of God will cause us to reject the sin; when we arduously fulfill a positive command even though there are grounds for exemption, we act out of love (R' Meyuchas).

As noted above, the name HASHEM represents His Attribute of Mercy, while Elohim [God] represents His Attribute of Strict Justice. The dual usage in this verse of HASHEM your God, implies: Whether He deals mercifully or strictly with you, in

1. The following treatment of the subject of the origins of Shema and the verse, Blessed be the Name of His glorious kingdom for all eternity, is taken from the footnote to the commentary of Genesis 49:1 in ArtScroll Bereishis:

In a discussion about the origins of the first verses of Shema, the Sages [Pesachim 56a] record the following tradition:

When Jacob wished to reveal the End of Days to his son, the Shechinah [Divine Presence] departed from him. Jacob grew frightened and mused: "Perhaps, Heaven forbid, there is someone unworthy among my children [lit., 'in my bed'], like Abraham who begot Ishmael, or like my father Isaac who begot Esau [and this is why the Shechinah left me when my children arrived]?"

Thereupon his sons reassured him: שְׁמַע יִשְׂרָאֵל ה' אֱלֹהֵינוּ ה' אֶחָד, Hear O Israel [i.e. our father] — HASHEM is our God, HASHEM is One! Just as there is only One in your heart, so is there only One in our heart."

[Although it is normally forbidden to address one's father by name, in this case it was permitted since the name Israel denotes greatness and authority (see Genesis 32:29) and as such it was more of a title than a name. It was as if they said, "Listen Master."]

At that moment Jacob, in relief that God's reason for denying them knowledge of the future was not because they lacked faith in Him ח"ו even to the slightest degree, exclaimed: בָּרוּךְ שֵׁם כְּבוֹד מַלְכוּתוֹ לְעוֹלָם וָעֶד, Blessed be the Name of His glorious kingdom for all eternity. [See Maharsha.]

The Talmudic discussion continues: The Sages pondered, Shall we say it? [I.e., shall we include the phrase בָּרוּךְ שֵׁם, blessed be the name, etc., during our daily recitations of Shema?] Moses our teacher did not. [That is, Moses did not include that phrase in the chapter of the Shema (Deut. 6:4-9). If Jacob's response were said in the Shema, we would be inserting something not written in the Torah.] However, Jacob did say it. [Therefore, if we exclude it, we would be ignoring Jacob's response to the first declaration of the Shema.] Accordingly the Sages established that the phrase בָּרוּךְ שֵׁם, Blessed be the Name etc., be recited silently [to make it apparent that it is not part of the Shema as written in the Torah but that it was uttered by Jacob (Mishnah Berurah 61:30 s.v. בְּחַשָׁאִי)].

One should pause briefly before beginning the next paragraph so as to make a distinction between the primary acceptance of God's Heavenly Kingdom, and acceptance of the commandments, which is the theme of the following, a theme he should bear in mind before beginning the paragraph:

Deuteronomy 6:5-9

⁵ You shall love HASHEM, your God, will all your heart and with all your soul and with all your resources.

either case, and in all ways: Love Him (*Alshich*).

One should have in mind that his love of God is absolute — even to the point of sacrificing all his desires, life, and possessions for God's sake (*Orach Chaim* 61).

◆§ **Love of HASHEM**

The obvious question arises: Since love is a matter of human emotion, how is it possible to legislate love when an individual cannot muster up such feeling? That God *does* demand this of us, however, proves that the ability to love is intrinsic to everyone. The duty devolves upon us to arouse this emotion and bring it from potentiality to reality. This, then, is the essence of this *mitzvah*: that we do anything necessary to remove the impediments and arouse our latent love of God (*Sfas Emes*).

According to *Rashi*, following *Sifre* [see next verse], the Torah itself tells us in the following verse how to achieve love of God: *Let these matters, which I command*

you today, be upon your heart — for thereby you will arrive at a recognition of HASHEM and will cling to His ways.

As *Rambam* explains: How can the Torah legislate love? — By contemplating God's greatness, the intricacy of His creation, and His simultaneous concern for the welfare of each insignificant creature, one can condition himself to love his Creator (*Yesodei HaTorah* 2:1-2). Thus, according to *Rambam*, love of God arises from intellectual conviction and from contemplation of God's greatness and His commandments, His words and His deeds. Thus, though the emotion of love is beyond man's control, by contemplation and study — activities that *are* subject to his will — man can attain love of Him.

Rambam pursues this theme further in his *Sefer HaMitzvos*, where he explains that this commandment also embodies the obligation that we should call upon all mankind to serve God and have faith in Him as Abraham did. For, "just as you recount the praises of someone you love and call upon other people to love him too,

Indeed, the halachah, as codified in *Shulchan Aruch* [ibid.] is that when reciting the *Shema* throughout the year we whisper the phrase *Blessed be* etc.

The only time this phrase is said aloud is on Yom Kippur. This custom is based on an alternate version of the declaration's origin. As *Tur* writes in *Hilchos Yom Kippur* §619:

It is the custom in Ashkenaz [i.e. Germany and the Eastern European countries] to recite בָּרוּךְ שֵׁם כְּבוֹד מַלְכוּתוֹ לְעוֹלָם וָעֶד in a loud voice on Yom Kippur. Support for this is in the Midrash, *Devarim Rabbah (Sidrah Va'eschanan)*, where it is written that 'when Moses ascended to heaven he heard the Ministering Angels praising God, "Blessed be the name of His glorious kingdom for all eternity," and Moses brought this declaration back to Israel. This may be compared to a man who stole jewelry from the royal palace [i.e., Moses 'stole' the declaration of the angels, as it were], which he gave to his wife, telling her, "Do not wear these in public, but only in the house." '

Therefore, concludes *Tur* citing the *Midrash*, "throughout the year we recite the declaration in a whisper, but on Yom Kippur when we are as pure as the Ministering Angels we recite it publicly [i.e. in a loud voice]."

[Comp. also *Devarim Rabbah* 2:31, according to which 'Blessed be, etc.' was Moses' response at Sinai to HASHEM'S exhortation: 'Hear O Israel, I am HASHEM your God ...' See also *Magen Avraham* 619 §8.]

R' Levi in *Devarim Rabbah* 2:35 also cites the view that Jacob's children reassured him of their faith by saying *Shema* as quoted above from *Pesachim* 56a. He remarks that when a Jew recites *Shema* nowadays, it is as if he says: 'Hear our father Israel: your command to our ancestors is still observed by us: HASHEM is our God, HASHEM is One!'

[Interestingly, in the Aramaic *Targum Yerushalmi* to our verse, Jacob's response to his sons' recitation of the *Shema* is given as יְהֵא שְׁמֵהּ רַבָּא מְבָרַךְ לְעָלַם וּלְעָלְמֵי עָלְמִין, 'May His Great Name be blessed forever and ever.' This response has been preserved as the primary response in the *Kaddish* prayer. See Overview to ArtScroll *Kaddish*.]

so it is that upon attaining true love of God and coming closer to a true understanding of His essence you will undoubtedly call upon the foolish and ignorant to seek a knowledge of the truth that you have already acquired."

In the words of the *Sifre*: [The commandment] *And you shall love HASHEM your God* implies that you should make Him beloved by man, as Abraham your father did. Just as Abraham, out of the strength of his convictions and of his great love for God, called upon mankind to believe in Him, so you are to love Him to the extent that you will call other men to Him.[1]

In his *Hilchos Teshuvah* [10:3,6], Rambam elaborates further on the emotional aspects of love of God:

What is the proper kind of love? It is that one should love HASHEM with such an exceedingly great and powerful love that his very soul be bound up in love of God. He will find himself constantly enraptured by it as if he were afflicted by the lovesickness of one who cannot clear his mind from passion for his beloved and he pines for her always, whether he sits or stands, whether he eats or drinks. Even greater than this should be the love of God in the hearts of those who love Him, enraptured by it always, as He commanded *with all your heart and with all your soul.* Solomon meant this allegorically when he said, "For I am lovesick" [Song of Songs 2, 5]. The whole *Song of Songs* is an allegory of man's love for God. [See Overview to ArtScroll *Shir HaShirim*, and *Hirhurei Teshuvah*.] It is well known and quite clear that love of the Holy One, Blessed is He,

cannot become established in the human heart until man is so completely enraptured by it that he neglects everything else on earth, as He commanded: *With all your heart and with all your soul.* One can love HASHEM only in proportion to the measure of the knowledge one has gained of Him. According to the knowledge so the love, whether less or more. Therefore man should devote himself to understanding and learning the wisdom and analytical skills that make his Maker known to him in accordance with his capacities as we have explained ... [see also *Yesodei HaTorah* 2:1.]

בְּכָל לְבָבְךָ — *With all your heart.* In Scriptural terminology, the 'heart' symbolizes man's intellectual spirit *(Ibn Ezra).*

By bidding us to love HASHEM with all the powers of our heart, our verse includes all the powers of the body since they all originate in the heart. The sense of the entire passage is: Make the perception of God the aim of all your actions *(Rambam, Moreh Nevuchim* 1:59). [See above: *Love of HASHEM.*]

The Sages in the Mishnah [*Berachos* 9:5] and *Sifre* note that the verse uses the לְבָב [with a double ב] for *heart* instead of the more familiar לֵב. From this they derive that we are bidden to love God with our 'double' heart. As *Rashi* explains: *With all your heart* — with both יֵצֶר הַטּוֹב וְיֵצֶר הָרָע, *the Good and Evil Inclinations.*

How can one love God with his inclination to do evil? — The true function of the Evil Inclination is to elevate man by providing him with a challenge to overcome.

Furthermore, even man's baser instincts — aspects of his Evil Inclination — must be

---

1. **Inspiring love by example**

The Talmud (*Yoma* 86a) perceives this obligation to love God in a broader sense. If one truly loves God, he will not be content to fulfill the commandments himself; he will act in such a way in all his daily activities with his fellow men that his actions will inspire others. Although our verse says only *And you shall love HASHEM your God,* the Sages expound that it means also that the Name of Heaven should become beloved through you [מִתְאָהֵב עַל יָדְךָ]. A Jew should study Scripture and Mishnah, and serve Torah scholars and deal graciously with his fellow creatures. Then his fellow creatures will say of him, 'Fortunate is his father who taught him Torah! Fortunate is his teacher who taught him Torah! Woe to those who do not study Torah! So and so who studies Torah — how pleasant is his behavior and how proper are his deeds. To him the verse applies: *And he said to me: You are My servant Israel, in whom I will be glorified'* (Isaiah 49:3).

However, if one studies Torah and Mishnah and serves Torah scholars, but is not honest in his dealings, does not converse pleasantly with people — what do people say of him? 'Woe to so and so who studies Torah! Woe to his father who taught him Torah! Pity his teacher who taught him Torah! So and so who studies Torah — see how corrupt are his deeds and how ugly his behavior! To him may the text be applied (*Ezek.* 36:20): *In that men said of them: These are HASHEM's people but they are departed from His land'* (*Yoma* 86a).

Similarly, *Sefer Chareidim* writes that included in the *mitzvah* of loving God is loving a Torah scholar who studies God's Word. The Talmud [*Shabbos* 23b] states that someone who loves Torah scholars will be blessed with children who are Torah scholars.

harnessed to serve God. All of man's earthly passions and ambitions must be made instruments in the service of God. Greed can be channeled to acquire money for charity; jealousy can goad one to greater efforts in his studies; hatred can be utilized to thwart God's enemies (R' Yonah to above Mishnah).

Alternately, Rashi interprets that expression with all your heart [the emphasis in this interpretation being on the word all] signifies: Your heart should not be at variance with God. [That is, do not be content merely to control your urges to sin. Instead, you should sublimate your urges to the point where your only desire is to love and serve God. You are to love Him with all your heart.]

Ramban cites the Midrashic opinion that heart figuratively refers to the power of desire. In the literal sense, however, he maintains that it denotes the rational soul — the intellect — 'since [in Scriptural terminology] the heart is the intellect's resting place.'

וּבְכָל נַפְשְׁךָ — And with all your soul. Soul figuratively refers to man's emotions; sometimes Scripture uses the term liver or innards as a metaphor for this concept. Specifically, soul in this context refers to man's will and desires [see this use in Gen. 23:8] and we are bidden to channel all our desires and emotions toward love of HASHEM (Ibn Ezra; Alshich).

Rashi, following the Talmudic Sages [Berachos 54a;61b; Sifre], interprets soul in its most literal sense as signifying life, and explains that our passage bids us to love God with total conviction and dedication — With all your soul — even if you must sacrifice your life for His sake [lit. even if He takes your soul].[1]

— "With every breath one breathes man is obligated to praise his Creator" (Midrash).

[In the vast majority of cases, however, the Torah commands Jews to put life ahead of the commandments. Thus, for example, work is done on the Sabbath where a life is at stake. The commandment to accept martyrdom for the sake of God applies only to the three cardinal sins — עֲבוֹדָה זָרָה, idolatry; גִּלּוּי עֲרָיוֹת, forbidden sexual union; and שְׁפִיכַת דָּמִים, murder — and to cases where commission of a sin would involve desecration of God's name. These principles are spelled out in Sanhedrin 74a and Yoreh Deah §157.]

Ramban notes the apparent superfluity in the word 'all' in this phrase. Following the Midrashic interpretation that your soul refers to martyrdom, what is signified by this additional word; one cannot speak of partial martyrdom? He suggests, accordingly, that suffering, or the sacrifice of bodily organs, is referred to as 'part of the soul,' while death is termed 'with all your soul.'

וּבְכָל מְאֹדֶךָ — And with all your resources. The translation follows the Talmud [Berachos 54a and 61b] and Rashi on Chumash: It means with all your money [or: property]. This command is added because there are people whose wealth is dearer to them than their own lives. [Accordingly, we must love God no matter what material sacrifice our loyalty entails, and whenever we recite these words we must bear in mind our willingness to submit to this test (Ibn Shu'ib).]

The Talmudic passage reads: If it says with all your soul, why should it also say with all your resources; and if it says with all your resources why should it say with all your soul? — Should there be a man who values his life more than his money, it tells him, with all your soul; and should there be a man who values his money more than his life, it tells him with all your resources.

1. R' Akiva's martyrdom while reciting the Shema

The classical example of loving God with one's last drop of blood is the Talmudic Sage, R' Akiva. He longed for the time when his daily acceptance of the obligation to love God might be put to the test and confirmed by action; when he was called upon to give his life for God's sake, would he be equal to the challenge? The moment came when he was arrested for publicly violating the Roman decree forbidding the Jews to study and teach the Torah, and was sentenced to death by torture.

When he was taken out for execution, it was the time for the recital of the Shema. While the Roman executioner tore his flesh with iron combs, R' Akiva was reciting the Shema, accepting upon himself the kingship of Heaven.

"Our teacher," his weeping disciples said, "even to this point?"

"All my days," R' Akiva told them, "I have been troubled by the passage with all your soul. I interpret it, 'even if He takes your soul,' and I have always longed for the opportunity of fulfilling this. Now that I have the opportunity of loving God with my whole life, should I not rejoice?"

R' Akiva prolonged the word echad until he died.

A Divine voice was heard proclaiming, "Happy are you, Akiva, that your soul departed with the word echad! …"

יְ וּבְכָל־מְאֹדֶךָ: וְהָיוּ הַדְּבָרִים הָאֵלֶּה אֲשֶׁר אָנֹכִי מְצַוְּךָ
ז הַיּוֹם עַל־לְבָבֶךָ: וְשִׁנַּנְתָּם לְבָנֶיךָ וְדִבַּרְתָּ בָּם בְּשִׁבְתְּךָ

Alternatively, *Rashi* cites the interpretation [ibid. 61b] that מְאֹד is related to the word מִדָּה, *measure*, and the phrase means: *And with all your 'measures.'* That is, your love for God should be undiminished no matter what measure [i.e. treatment] He deals out to you — whether He treats you generously or not.

— Love God in times of bliss and happiness and in times of stress and misfortune. While we recite these words we must concentrate on our gracious acceptance of the treatment God subjects us to (*Ibn Shu'ib*).

It is from our passage that the Talmudic Sages [*Berachos* 54a] derive the dictum: "חַיָּיב אָדָם לְבָרֵךְ עַל־הָרָעָה כְּשֵׁם שֶׁמְּבָרֵךְ עַל הַטּוֹבָה, *It is incumbent on a man to bless God for the evil in the same way as for the good.*"[1]

Following the primary interpretation that the word מְאֹד refers to *wealth*, the *Vilna Gaon* used to render the passage homiletically: *You shall serve HASHEM ... even with all your possessions* — that is, even if

you are very wealthy.

Ibn Ezra and *Ramban* interpret the term as deriving from מְאֹד, *much*, the passage meaning love Him *very, very much* — with all your intensity of feeling. *Ramban* cites the Rabbinic interpretation (quoted above) that it means *with all your resources*, since one's property is called מְאֹד, *abundance* ... and the *mitzvah* is to love Him "with all the abundance of your wealth."

The use of the term מְאֹד [*much*] to imply *resources* rather than more common terms, such as קִנְיָן, *possessions;* רְכוּשׁ, *wealth;* or כֶּסֶף, *money*, connotes that more than financial resources is meant. It refers to anything to which an individual might be closely attached. Even *that* must be sacrificed when love of God is at stake (*Chofetz Chaim*).

However, while we are bidden to forfeit all our resources rather than violate a prohibition of the Torah, we are not required to sacrifice more than a fifth of our resources in order to fulfill a positive commandment (see *Orach Chaim* 8696).[2]

1. Two brothers, Rabbis Pinchas and Shmelka Horowitz, who later became very distinguished chassidic leaders, came to the Maggid (preacher) of Mezritch to inquire about the nature of Chassidic philosophy and teaching. During their discussion, they asked him to explain how it was possible to thank God equally for good and for bad. To that, the Maggid replied, 'Go to my Zussia, he will answer you.'

Rabbi Zussia of Anipoli was a disciple who spent most of his day in the Maggid's study hall. He was poverty-stricken, in constant pain from a variety of physical maladies, and his wife was a notorious shrew. Nevertheless, R' Zussia was famous for his unvarying good cheer. The two visiting brothers went to him and asked their question, telling him that the Maggid had directed them to him.

R' Zussia seemed dumbfounded. He said, 'That is a difficult question, but I cannot imagine why the Maggid sent you to me. Only someone who has experienced suffering and problems can answer such a question. I, thank God, have always had a good life with everything I need!'

Then the two rabbis understood what the Maggid meant. A person should always be so joyous that he accepts whatever God metes out to him with the same grateful acknowledgment.

2. This phrase *with all your resources* only occurs in this portion of *Shema*, which is addressed in singular to individuals. However, the second section, וְהָיָה, which is worded in plural to the community, omits this concept of sacrificing all community resources for God's sake. This is because the entire community's preservation of property and the means of earning a livelihood are matters of life and death, and as such are included in וּבְכָל נַפְשְׁכֶם, *and with all your souls* [p. 33 below] (*Rabbi of Kotzk*).

Rabbi Zalman Sorotzkin (*Oznaim LaTorah*) discusses this concept, explaining a basic difference between the entire community and its members. Even if an individual gives up all his resources and his means of a livelihood for the sake of God, he is not without hope because he can rely on the community to come to his assistance, as has happened countless times throughout Jewish history. When an individual is asked to serve God with all his *resources*, he knows that his *life* is not at stake; therefore he must be instructed further that, if need be, even his life should be forfeit if necessary. For an entire community to become destitute, however, is far more serious than a mere matter of economics. Without resources and a means of earning them — and without the community to help them — utter poverty can mean disease and starvation. Therefore, the second section's command that even a community must serve God with all his resources is tantamount to telling them that they must be ready even to give up their livelihood if need be. [See Second Portion p. 33 for additional reasons.]

⁶Let these matters which I command you this day, be upon your heart. ⁷ Teach them thoroughly to your children and speak of them while you sit in your home, while you walk

6. How are we to achieve the 'love' of God demanded of us in the previous verse? — The following verse tells us: *Let these words which I command you today be upon your heart* — for by constant absorption with the words of Torah, you will arrive at a recognition of God and will cling to His way *(Sifre; Rashi).*

Thus, this passage advocates diligent Torah-study, since that will lead to proper love of God *(Haamek Davar).* [See above: "Love of HASHEM."]

וְהָיוּ הַדְּבָרִים הָאֵלֶּה — *And let these matters* [lit. *and these words shall be*].

These words: either the words of this chapter, mandating love of God, or the *mitzvos* of the Torah in general (see *Mizrachi; Gur Aryeh; R' Hirsch; Haamek Davar.* See also *HaKsav V'HaKabbalah* who goes to great length to stress that the emphasis is on the *mitzvah* of loving God mandated in this chapter).

The Rabbis in the Talmud variously interpret that the expression וְהָיוּ, *and they shall be*, implies that 'they must remain as they are.' This teaches that one who recites the *Shema* fulfills his obligation only if the words are recited in the order in which they are written *(Berachos 13a).*

אֲשֶׁר אָנֹכִי מְצַוְּךָ הַיּוֹם — *Which I command you this day.* The word הַיּוֹם, *this day,* carries with it a sublime message beyond the literal connotation: Do not regard the Divine commands as old and obsolete; but regard them as eternally fresh, like a new royal proclamation reaching you this very day [which all cheerfully obey because it

denotes that the monarch had but that very day expressed his will] *(Rashi; Sifre).*[1]

While reciting the *Shema*, one must be careful to pause between the word הַיּוֹם, *today,* and the following phrase עַל לְבָבֶךָ, *upon your heart*, so it not appear as if the verse implied: let it be upon your heart only *today* — but not other days *(Shulchan Aruch;* see *Pesachim* 56a).

עַל-לְבָבֶךָ — *Be upon your heart.* The intent of *upon your heart* is that these words should govern your heart, i.e., that you be in charge of your emotions and not *vice versa (R' Menachem Mendel of Kalish).*

— In the literal sense: You should always be prepared to fulfill these words *(R' Hoffmann).*

This is the method of attaining love of God. If one remains *always* conscious of the teachings of the Torah and of his obligations to God, he will inevitably come to love Him *(Sifre).*

— The teachings should figuratively *lay upon your heart* like a stone, and when, in a propitious moment of inspiration, the heart "opens" receptively, then these words will enter it directly *(R' Menachem Mendel of Kotzk).*

7. וְשִׁנַּנְתָּם לְבָנֶיךָ — *[And] teach them thoroughly to your children.*[2] Literally the verb signifies 'impress sharply.' The words of the Torah shall be 'sharp' [i.e. familiar] in your mouth, so that if a person asks you anything concerning them you will not stammer but will answer immediately *(Kiddushin 30a; Rashi).*

Rashi thereby maintains that וְשִׁנַּנְתָּם is derived

1. Everyone must view himself as if he were the only person in the universe; as if God's commands applied to him only; as if the Torah were the only Book he had; and as if that day were his last. In this way, one will certainly not waste a precious moment in his service to God and performance of *mitzvos.* This is the implication of our verse: "*And let these matters* — of This Torah, which is the only Book you possess, *which I command you* — you specifically, *this day* — only this day do you have the ability to heed My words for by the morrow you might no longer be alive" *(Chofetz Chaim).*

2. The *Chidushei HaRim* had thirteen children, all of whom died in his lifetime. He resolutely withstood all of these tragedies shedding hardly a tear, but would merely say, "HASHEM has given and HASHEM has taken away."

When his last child died, however, he could not maintain his composure, but wept bitterly and uncontrollably. One of his close chassidim asked him why on his earlier losses he was able to control his emotions whereas here he was unable to do so.

"I am weeping over one thing," the Rebbe said, "that henceforth I will be unable to fulfill the *mitzvah* of וְשִׁנַּנְתָּם לְבָנֶיךָ, *teach them thoroughly to your children.*"

בְּבֵיתֶ֖ךָ וּבְלֶכְתְּךָ֣ בַדֶּ֑רֶךְ וּֽבְשָׁכְבְּךָ֖ וּבְקוּמֶֽךָ׃ וּקְשַׁרְתָּ֛ם ח

from the verb שנן, *sharpen*, rather than from the verb שנה, *teach* [as in מִשְׁנָה]. [*Rashbam, Ibn Ezra* and other commentators concur.] The passage would accordingly be contextually rendered: *And you shall master them thoroughly for the sake of your children* (*Mizrachi; Tzeidah laDerech*).

Rashi continues that the word *children* refers [also] to students. Furthermore, just as the word *children* can be extended to denote *students*, so the term אָב [*father*] can be extended to denote a *teacher*.

The commentators explain that *Rashi* is drawn to this interpretation that *children* in our context refers to *students* because the obligation upon a father to teach Torah to his sons and grandsons was stated explicitly several verses earlier in the Torah [*Deut.* 4:9]. Thus, *Rashi* pursues the interpretation that this verse has the more general application that it is incumbent upon everyone to transmit Torah knowledge to disciples (*Maskil l'David*).

וְדִבַּרְתָּ בָּם — *And speak of them.* Your *principal* topic of conversation should be about them [i.e. the Words of Torah]: they should not be relegated to secondary importance (*Rashi*).

By constantly reviewing your Torah knowledge, you will not forget it. Memory is best preserved by a constant verbal repetition. Hence the precept that one should *speak* of the Divine commandments (*Sforno*).

They are to be a theme of living interest, early and late, at home and abroad. This does not exclude other talk entirely; rather, as *Rashi* stresses, we are exhorted that Torah topics form our *principal* conversation (*Gur Aryeh*).

[*Rashi's* interpretation follows one view in the Talmud (*Yoma* 19a); there is another view cited there, however, that this passage enjoins us not to engage in idle and loose talk.]

According to Talmud *Yerushalmi Sotah* 7:1 we derive from this verse — which is interpreted to imply: בְּכָל לָשׁוֹן שֶׁאַתָּה מְדַבֵּר, *in every language that you speak* — that the *Shema* may be recited in any language (if one does not understand Hebrew [see *Berachos* 13a cited in *comm.* to *Shema.* Cf. *Torah Temimah*].

בְּשָׁבְתְּךָ בְּבֵיתֶךָ וּבְלֶכְתְּךָ בַדֶּרֶךְ — *While you sit in your home, while you walk on the way.* — That is, during, [and in the manner of] your usual course of living [see below] (*Rashi*).

Even when one is pursuing his usual daily activities, and his mind is preoccupied with the business at hand, even then he should focus his thought on whatever Torah matters he can meditate upon at that moment (*Etz Yosef*).

◆§ The time for reading Shema

וּֽבְשָׁכְבְּךָ וּבְקוּמֶךָ — [*And*] *when you recline and when you arise.* [This passage is not merely figurative; it refers to the mandated reading of the *Shema* in the evening and in the morning.] *Rashi* explains that the reference to 'reclining and arising' is not to imply that the time of reciting *Shema* depends on an *individual's* personal habits — for example it does not apply to one who reclines [i.e., naps] in the middle of the day or who arises in the middle of the night. Rather, our verse refers to the *usual* manner of things. The requirement to recite *Shema* applies to the *customary* times of retiring and awakening.

[This passage is the subject of halachic controversy between the schools of Shammai and Hillel (*Berachos* 10b). According to the former, the words *recline* and *arise* are to be interpreted literally: in the evening one should recline while reciting the *Shema*, and in the morning one should stand. The disciples of Hillel disagree. They deduce from וּבְלֶכְתְּךָ בַדֶּרֶךְ, *and while you walk on the way,* that one reads *Shema* כְּדַרְכּוֹ, *in his natural manner,* whether walking, sitting, or standing. If so our phrase cannot place a requirement on reclining or standing; hence the phrase refers to the *time* when the *Shema* is to be recited — viz. in the evening when people *generally* recline and in the morning when people *generally* arise (see below). The Halachah follows the latter view, and *Rashi* accordingly bases his interpretation on it.]

The time for reciting the night-*Shema* is all night — from the time the stars become visible [צֵאת הַכּוֹכָבִים], until *daybreak* [עֲלוֹת הַשַּׁחַר]. However, the Sages ordained that it should be recited before midnight, lest someone fall asleep and forget to recite it. The time for reciting the day-*Shema* begins from the time there is enough daylight for someone to recognize a comrade from a distance of about four cubits [about eight feet] until a quarter of the daylight hours have passed.

on the way, when you recline and when you arise. ⁸ Bind
them as a sign upon your arm and they shall be tefillin

◆§ The ritual

The ritual of the evening *Shema* consists of the three sections of the *Shema* preceded by two benedictions and followed by another two. Of the preliminary benedictions, the first refers to the Divine ordering of day and night, הַמַּעֲרִיב עֲרָבִים; and the second describes the love of God shown by the giving of the Torah, אַהֲבַת עוֹלָם. Of the benedictions following the *Shema*, the first is a proclamation of faith, אֱמֶת וֶאֱמוּנָה; and the second, a prayer for peaceful repose, הַשְׁכִּיבֵנוּ. The Evening Service continues with the *Amidah*, and *Aleinu*. [The benediction בָּרוּךְ ה' לְעוֹלָם was added in later times.] The *Shema* is also recited — with the addition of certain psalms and benedictions — before retiring to sleep [see pp. 48-62].

The morning *Shema* is preceded by two benedictions, and followed by one. These Benedictions are (1): Praise of God as the Creator of the light of day, יוֹצֵר אוֹר; (2) Praise of God as Giver of the Torah, אַהֲבָה רַבָּה; and (3) Praise of God as the Redeemer of Israel, גָּאַל יִשְׂרָאֵל. Immediately thereafter in the morning service comes the *Amidah*.

◆§ Tefillin

8. וּקְשַׁרְתָּם לְאוֹת עַל־יָדֶךָ — *[And you shall]* bind them [i.e., the words of this section along with the other sections mandated by Halachah] *as a sign upon your arm.*

[This is not merely figurative.] — It refers to the *tefillin* for the arm *(Rashi).*

[The term *tefillin* (commonly rendered with the Greek word, *phylacteries*) — singular *tefillah* — derives from the root פלל, having the connotation of *prayer* (Hebrew: *tefillah*), *judgment* [*Psalms* 106:30] and *testimony*. See *Tosafos Menachos* 34b s.v. לְטוֹטָפֹת; *Tur Orach Chaim* 25; *Shorashim* s.v. פלל; comm. to *Ezekiel* 24:17 s.v. פְּאֵרְךָ where *Targum Yonasan* interprets that word as טֹטָפְתָּךְ. See below on טֹטָפֹת.]

The *mitzvah* 562 of *tefillin* had already been mentioned in *Exodus* 13:9, but here the Torah clarifies that the *tefillin* are to be *bound* on the arm and head *(Ramban).*

Tefillin contain four paragraphs: קַדֶּשׁ *(Exodus* 13:1-10); וְהָיָה כִּי יְבִאֲךָ *(ibid.* 11-

16); שְׁמַע *(Deut.* 4-8); וְהָיָה אִם שָׁמֹעַ *(ibid.* 11:13-21).

Ramban and *Chinuch* explain that these four sections were chosen in preference to all other passages of the Torah because they embrace the acceptance of Heavenly sovereignty, the precept of the Unity of God, the acceptance of His commandments with the acknowledgment that they involve reward and punishment, and the Exodus from Egypt — all fundamental doctrines of Judaism. Furthermore, the law of *tefillin* is mentioned in these four sections.

For the *tefillin* on the arm, the four paragraphs are written on one strip of parchment and housed in a single case, but for the *tefillin* of the head, the four paragraphs are written on separate pieces of parchment and placed into a case divided into four compartments. This is exegetically derived from the *singular* word אוֹת, *sign*, associated with the hand *tefillin*, and the *plural* טֹטָפֹת, [meaning *four* (see *Rashi* below)] associated with the head *tefillin*. The laws of the construction of *tefillin* were transmitted to Moses at Sinai הֲלָכָה לְמֹשֶׁה מִסִּינַי (see *Menachos* 34-36).

The commentators explain that *tefillin* is one of the commandments that are like emblems identifying us as God's servants. Just as royal officials wear uniforms and insignia that distinguish them from others and remind them constantly of their duty to the sovereign, so too the Jew is set apart by such insignia. Among them are circumcision in his flesh, *tefillin* on his head and arm, *tzitzis* on his garment, and *mezuzah* on his doorpost. They are constantly visible reminders, pointing his way wherever he goes and whatever he does, proclaiming that an Eye from which he cannot hide sees his every deed.

In ancient times *tefillin* were worn throughout the day; nowadays their use is generally confined to morning prayers.

◆§ Position of the hand-tefillin

The word יָד can be rendered either *arm* (including the hand) or *hand*, depending on the context [see *Arachin* 19b; *Tos. Menachos* 37a s.v. קְבוּרַת], although in common usage it has come to be used nearly always for *hand*. *Tosefta (Shabbos*

ט לְאוֹת עַל־יָדֶךָ וְהָיוּ לְטֹטָפֹת בֵּין עֵינֶיךָ: וּכְתַבְתָּם עַל־
מְזֻזוֹת בֵּיתֶךָ וּבִשְׁעָרֶיךָ:

9:15) proves from *Judges* 15:14 that the entire arm is called יָד (see also *Malbim* to *Mechilta, Bo* §110). In the case of *tefillin*, עַל יָדְךָ must be rendered *upon your arm* — not *upon your hand* — since the Talmud [*Menachos ibid.* and *Sifre*] derives that the hand-*tefillin* must be bound on the inner biceps muscle — opposite the heart. [See comm. to parallel phrase in Second Portion, v. 18, s.v. וּקְשַׁרְתָּם p. 38.] Thus, it is not "on the *hand*" but on the muscle of the *upper arm*, which controls the entire organ. This also conforms with the parallel text in *Exodus* 13:9 where the hand-*tefillin* are to be לְךָ לְאוֹת, *to you a sign*, i.e. a *personal* sign visible to the wearer alone [on the part of the arm usually covered by the sleeve] rather than on the "*hand*" — where it would be seen by all. The head-*tefillin*, however, are to be seen by all (*Menachos ibid.*). [See *B'chor Shor* below בֵּין עֵינֶיךָ.]

The *arm* on which the *tefillin* is to be put is the left one. The Sages expound this in two ways. First, when this commandment is given in *Exodus* 13:6, the word יָדְךָ is spelled יָדְכָה [=יַד כֵּהָה 'weak arm'] implying the left, which is the weaker of the two hands. The second derivation of this law is from the proximity to one another of two words: וּקְשַׁרְתָּם, *and you shall bind them* in our verse, and וּכְתַבְתָּם, *and you shall write them*, in the next verse. The Talmud, *Menachos* 37a, interprets: "Just as writing is with the right hand so the binding must be done with the right." Since one must use his right hand to bind the hand-*tefillin*, it must be put on the left arm. [There is also an exposition in *Menachos* 36b based upon *Isaiah* 48:13, *Judges* 5:26, and *Psalms* 74:11 where *hand* clearly means left hand.]

According to both derivations, a left-handed person would put *tefillin* on his right hand, because his right arm is weaker and because he writes and binds with his left hand.

Inasmuch as *tefillin* are referred to as אוֹת, *sign* [see especially *Exodus* 13:16], the Sages derive that *tefillin* are not worn on Sabbaths and festivals, because these sacred days are themselves referred to as 'signs' between God and Israel. [See *Exod.* 31:13 and *comm.*] (*Eruvin* 96a; see *Torah Sheleimah*).

Shulchan Aruch cites the custom that while saying the words וּקְשַׁרְתָּם לְאוֹת עַל־יָדְךָ [during *Shacharis* services], one should touch the *tefillin* of the arm, and while saying the words וְהָיוּ לְטֹטָפֹת בֵּין עֵינֶיךָ, touch the *tefillin* of the head. Some have the custom of kissing the fingers after touching the *tefillin*.

וְהָיוּ לְטֹטָפֹת בֵּין עֵינֶיךָ — *And they shall be [for] tefillin between your eyes.*
— A reference to the *tefillin* for the head (*Rashi*).

◄§ **Position of the head-tefillin**

The expression "**between** your eyes," as it is used in Scripture, refers to the front part of the skull, *above the center-point between the eyes.* This definition is derived from *Deuteronomy* 14:1, as explained below. Thus, the head-*tefillin* are to be placed between the hairline and the spot toward the upper part of the head where the skull of a baby is still tender. [See *Menachos* 37a,b.] That they are placed above the hairline is derived from another law that involves a comparison with *Deuteronomy* 14:1. There we are enjoined from excessive manifestations of mourning: *You shall not cut yourselves nor make a bald patch between your eyes for the dead.* Obviously, that verse does not mean literally *between your eyes,* for no hair grows there. Rather, both verses designate a place above the hairline on the anterior part of the skull — "the seat of the organ from which the eyes are controlled and the impressions of the thoughts they gather are received" (*R' Hirsch*).

"There is no doubt regarding the interpretation [that *upon your* **hand** and *between your* eyes refer respectively to the inner part of the upper arm against the heart, and to the anterior part of the skull] ... So have we received the tradition from our Rabbis, and so have our forefathers done. Whoever casts doubts upon this is like one who would question that the letter א is called *aleph* rather than *beth*, and they will in the future be summoned to render judgment" (*B'chor Shor*).

The *mitzvah* of *tefillin* is mentioned earlier in *Exodus*, in two almost identical passages: *Exodus* 13:9, *And it shall be as a "sign" for you upon your hand, and as a*

סדר קריאת שמע [28]

between your eyes. ⁹ And write them on the doorposts of
your house and upon your gates.

"memorial" between your eyes; and *ibid.,
v. 16, And it shall be as a "sign" for you
upon your hand, and as "tefillin"* [Hebrew:
totafos (see below)] *between your eyes.*

Ramban to Exod. ibid. explains that the
expression *as a "memorial"* [לְזִכָּרוֹן]
between your eyes implies that the head-
tefillin are to be placed at the "seat of
remembrance," high above the eyes at the
beginning of the brain. The expression
"between [בֵּין] *the eyes"* indicates that they
are to be placed on the *middle* of the head
not toward the side.

◄§ Hand-tefillin before head-tefillin

Since the hand-*tefillin* is mentioned first,
the *halachah* is that the hand-*tefillin* must
be put on before the head-*tefillin.*
However, the head-*tefillin* is to be removed
first, then the hand-*tefillin.* The latter law
is derived from our passage, which is
expounded *(Menachos* 36a) to imply that
whenever the head-*tefillin* is worn, it must
be worn in tandem with the hand-*tefillin.*
In connection with the head-*tefillin,* our
verse uses the plural expression וְהָיוּ, **they
shall be.** This implies that whenever the
head-*tefillin* are worn, *both tefillin* should
be on the body. Consequently, it should be
put on last and taken off first (see *Rashi ad
loc.* and *Torah Temimah).*

◄§ Meaning of the word טֹטָפֹת

The etymology of the word טֹטָפֹת is
obscure. It occurs in the Torah only here,
in the parallel phrase in *Deut.* 13:18, and in
Exodus 13:9 where the *mitzvah* of *tefillin* is
first mentioned.

The translation of טֹטָפֹת as *tefillin*
follows *Onkelos,* and *Rashi* to *Exod.* 13:16.
Rashi quotes the Talmudic derivation
[*Sanhedrin* 4b] that the word is a
compound of the foreign words *tot* and *pas*
— each being a numeral meaning *two,* the
one in the language of Katpi [Caspian;
Coptic(?)] and the other in the language of
Afriki [a district of North Africa;
Phrygian(?)]. He explains that *tefillin* are so
called because the head-*tefillin* consists of
four compartments.

Abarbanel suggests that the word may
be derived from the old Egyptian word *tot*
or *otat,* meaning brain, the organ above

which the head-*tefillin* are placed
(*Abarbanel*).

Onkelos renders the term as *tefillin* rather
than the Aramaic equivalent, *totafos,* because
Onkelos customarily preserves the familiar
meaning of a term, in this case, *tefillin,* rather
than the strict literal sense of the word. [That the
Aramaic word for *tefillin* is *totafos* is evident
from *Ezekiel* 24:17 where the Hebrew adjective
for *tefillin,* פְּאֵר, *majesty,* is rendered in the
Targum as טוֹטַפְתָּךְ.] *Onkelos* acted similarly in
Leviticus 23:40 where he does not translate the
following terms literally but gives them their
traditional *halachic* meaning: פְּרִי עֵץ הָדָר [fruit
of a goodly tree]=*esrog;* כַּפֹּת תְּמָרִים [branches of
palm trees]=*lulav;* עֲנַף עֵץ־עָבֹת [boughs of thick
trees]=*hadasim;* עַרְבֵי נַחַל [brook
willows]=*aravos (Marpei Lashon; Shaarei
Aharon).*

In an alternative interpretation, *Rashi* [in
Exodus ibid.] quotes the grammarian
Menachem ben Saruk who derives the
word from the root נטף, *to speak* [see
Ezekiel 21:2; *Micah* 2:6]; hence *totafos* is
something that inspires conversation, and
is the equivalent of the parallel expression
memorial in *Exodus* 13:9. That is, the
head-*tefillin* will serve as a reminder of
God's miracles, and inspire all who see it to
speak about them.

Ramban maintains that in the literal
sense the Sages [*Shabbos* 57a] understood
the word טֹטָפֹת as denoting an ornament
worn over the forehead extending from ear
to ear, as they have ruled in the Mishnah
[ibid.]: "A woman may not go out on the
Sabbath with a *totefes* or head-bangles [i.e.
frontlets]." He writes that since the Sages
spoke and knew the language of Scripture,
we can well accept their definition. [See
also *Targum* to *II Samuel* 1:10.] That the
Torah employs the plural term *totafos*
rather than the singular *totefes* is because
the head-*tefillin* contains several compartments. These compartments have the form
and arrangement that we have received
from our forebears, who in turn saw the
prophets and ancient ones acting the same
way, in a tradition dating back to Moses at
Sinai ... *Tefillin* on the arm, next to the
heart, symbolizes that all one's strength
and passions are dedicated to God, while
tefillin on the head symbolizes dedication
to Him of the intellect.

This is one of the verses that parallels

one of the Ten Commandments: *You shall not covet your neighbor's house.* Our passage accordingly specifies בֵּיתֶךְ, 'your house,' not your neighbor's house, implying that one should be content with his own lot and not be envious of his neighbor's. See p. 63.

9. The law of Mezuzah

וּכְתַבְתָּם עַל מְזֻזוֹת בֵּיתֶךָ וּבִשְׁעָרֶיךָ — *And write them on the doorposts of your house and upon [lit. in] your gates.* This commandment is fulfilled by affixing a *mezuzah*-scroll to each doorpost in Jewish houses. Literally, the word *mezuzah* means *doorpost* [see *Exodus* 12:7, 22, 23; and 21:6]. Although this passage would seem to require that one should write the words directly on the doorpost, the Sages in *Menachos* 34a teach that they are to be written on a scroll. This is derived by means of a *gezeirah shavah* (see footnote above) from the fact that the verb כתב, *write*, is used also in connection with the law of a bill of divorce [*Deut.* 24:1], where the writing must be done on a scroll [cf. *Tosafos*]; similarly in the case of *mezuzah*, the writing must be done on a scroll in the prescribed manner and affixed to the doorpost. According to another view there in the Talmud this teaching is derived from the word וּכְתַבְתָּם, *and you shall write them*, which alludes to a כְּתִיבָה תַּמָּה, *perfectly distinct writing.* That is, the Hebrew וּכְתַבְתָּם is interpreted as though it were two words וּכְתַב תָּם, *write perfectly*, and this can be accomplished only when writing with ink upon a scroll, for, as the commentators explain, any writing with ink directly upon a doorpost of wood, brick, or stone would be imperfect and indistinct.

Thus, although the word *mezuzah* means doorpost in Scriptural Hebrew, in popular usage it has come to refer to the *scroll*, rather than to the doorpost itself.

The *mezuzah* contains the first two sections of *Shema*: שְׁמַע and וְהָיָה אִם שָׁמֹעַ written in the manner of letters of the Torah scroll, traditionally in 22 lines. Both of these sections contain references to the law of *mezuzah* in their final verses. On the back of the parchment the Name שַׁדַּי ("Almighty," but also, according to *Kol Bo*, the initial letters of שׁוֹמֵר דַּלְתוֹת יִשְׂרָאֵל, *Guardian of the doors of Israel*) is written, and the parchment is inserted into its case so that the word is visible through an aperture in the case.

At the bottom of the blank side, the letters כוזו במוכסז כוזו are also written, which, according to the Kabbalistic alphabetical system in which every letter alludes the preceding one, reads: ה' אלהינו ה', *HASHEM, our God, HASHEM.* The rolled up parchment is affixed to the right-hand doorpost of every room, house, or gate, in the top third of the doorpost and slanting inward. It is customary to touch the *mezuzah* reverently and kiss the fingers that touched it whenever entering or leaving a house.

When one enters the house, he touches the *mezuzah* to remind himself that he is treading upon consecrated ground; when he leaves, he touches it to commit his house to the protection of God to Whom it is dedicated (*R' Hirsch, Choreb*; see *Yoreh Deah* 285).

That the *mezuzah* is affixed to the upper third of the doorpost is derived in the Talmud [*Menachos* 33a] from the proximity of the phrases וּקְשַׁרְתָּם ... וּכְתַבְתָּם, *and you shall bind them ... and you shall write them.* Just as the binding of the *tefillin* is 'high up' [on the arm, and toward the top of the head], so must the 'writing' be placed high up, on the top third of the doorpost.

That the *mezuzah* is to be affixed to the *right* doorpost is derived in the Talmud [*ibid.* 34a] from the expression *'on the doorposts* בֵּיתֶךָ *of your house'* which is interpreted to imply בִּיאָתֶךָ, *as you enter*, i.e., on the right side, since one steps into a house with his right foot first. Another Sage in the Talmud derives it from *II Kings* 12:10, which reads ... *on the right side as one comes into the house of HASHEM.*

Another exegesis derived from this phrase is that *'your' house* refers to the one who lives there; thus, the responsibility for affixing a *mezuzah* to a dwelling rests with the tenant, rather than the landlord.

Basing himself on some early Midrashim that are at variance with the Masoretic text, and according to which the word מְזֻזוֹת in our passage is spelled 'defectively' without the ו [see *Minchas Shay* to *Exodus* 12:7], *Rashi* comments: The word is spelled מזוזת [which in the unvowelized Torah can be read as if it were in the singular מְזֻזַת]. This indicates that it is necessary to affix only one *mezuzah* to a doorpost. [Cf. *Menachos* 34a; *Sifsei Chachomim*; and *HaKsav V'Hakabalah.*]

◆§ Purpose of Mezuzah

The *mezuzah* is a symbol that all of man's possessions belong to God Who, in His graciousness, granted them to us, and that it is prohibited for one to enjoy them until he offers thanks and blessing to their

Giver. Since man's primary possession is his home, God commanded that a *mezuzah* be attached to the various doorposts, so that every time one enters and leaves a room one will recall God to Whom all property belongs, and realize that all is His, and man should not glory in his own wealth since all is Divinely bestowed *(Iyun Tefillah).*

Furthermore, throughout Talmudic, Kabbalistic and Rabbinic literature we find many references to the fact that the sacred words of the *mezuzah* have a mystical protective power to ward off evil from the home on which it is affixed and its occupants.[1]

Aruch HaShulchan cautions, however, that this aspect of the *mezuzah* should not form a person's primary intention in fulfilling the precept. Rather one must fulfill it because it is God's Will, and the reward will inevitably follow.

Finally, as *Ramban* writes in his conclusion to the laws of *mezuzah* [6:13]: A person should be scrupulous regarding the precept of the *mezuzah;* for it is an eternal obligation binding upon everyone. Whenever one enters or leaves a home, he will encounter the Declaration of the Unity of the Name of the Holy One, Blessed is He, and will recall the love due Him, and will be aroused from his slumber and his preoccupation with transitory vanities. He will realize that nothing endures forever except for knowledge of the Rock of the Universe. Then he will return at once to his proper senses and he will walk the paths of the righteous. Our early Sages said [*Menachos* 33a]: "Whoever has *tefillin* on his head and arm, *tzitzis* on his garment, and a *mezuzah* on his door is assured not to sin, for he has many to remind him — angels that rescue him from sinning, as it is said *(Psalms 34:8): The angel of HASHEM encamps round those that fear Him, and delivers them.*"

The term וּבִשְׁעָרֶיךָ, *and upon your gates,* extends the obligation of affixing a *mezuzah* to the gates of courtyards, provinces, and cities *(Rashi; Yoma* 10a).

Based on the term *'and in your gates,'* *Haamek Davar* suggests that on public gateways it is proper to chisel out an area on the post for the *mezuzah*, so that it can be recessed. While it is permitted to mount a *mezuzah* on the surface, nevertheless it is advisable to recess it. Inside a home, where cleanliness is assured, it is better for the *mezuzah* to be visible; however, on public gates, where cleanliness cannot be guaranteed, it is best for the *mezuzah* to be recessed and concealed.

◆§ The Second Portion [*Deut.* 11:13-21].

Acceptance of the Commandments. *The reward for the fulfillment of the mitzvos; the punishment for their transgression; reiteration of the contents of the first portion.*

Regarding the sequence of the portions of the *Shema,* the *Mishnah* [*Berachos* 13a] states: "Why was the section of שְׁמַע placed before that of וְהָיָה אִם שָׁמֹעַ — So that one should first accept upon himself עוֹל מַלְכוּת שָׁמַיִם, *God's absolute sovereignty* [by proclaiming His unity], and then accept upon himself the עוֹל הַמִּצְוֹת, *the yoke of the commandments*" [by the passage: *If you shall hearken diligently to all My commandments*].

Most of this section is in the plural inasmuch as it speaks of the performance of the commandments, which is preferably done in public. The Sages have said [*Yalkut Beha'aloscha*] "One cannot compare communal performance to private performance." [See *Rashi* to *v.* 13 below.]

In the Scriptural context: In the Biblical verses preceding this message [*Deut.* 11:10ff], Moses continues his farewell exhortation to the Jewish people to heed God's commands

---

1. Talmud [*Avodah Zarah* 11a] relates a story of Onkelos, a Roman noble who converted to Judaism. His relative, the Roman Emperor, sent a succession of troops to arrest him for his conversion, but Onkelos succeeded in convincing all to convert. Finally, the emperor sent a company with strict orders not to allow Onkelos to engage them in conversation.

The ploy succeeded but, as they were escorting Onkelos out of the house, he looked at the *mezuzah* on his doorpost, placed his hand upon it, and said: "I will tell you what this is. The universal custom is for a human king to sit inside a room with his servants guarding him from the outside. With the Holy One, Blessed is He, however, His servants are inside a room and He guards them from the outside [by means of the *mezuzah*], *as it is said [Psalms 121:8]: HASHEM will guard your leaving and your entering henceforth and forevermore.*" When the Roman soldiers heard that, they too converted, and the emperor stopped his attempts to arrest Onkelos.

One should bear in mind before reciting the next paragraph that he is about to declare
his belief in the principle of reward and punishment.

יג וְהָיָ֗ה אִם־שָׁמֹ֤עַ תִּשְׁמְעוּ֙ אֶל־מִצְוֺתַ֔י אֲשֶׁ֧ר אָנֹכִ֛י
מְצַוֶּ֥ה אֶתְכֶ֖ם הַיּ֑וֹם לְאַהֲבָ֞ה אֶת־יהוה
יד אֱלֹֽהֵיכֶם֙ וּלְעָבְד֔וֹ בְּכָל־לְבַבְכֶ֖ם וּבְכָל־נַפְשְׁכֶֽם: וְנָתַתִּ֧י

lest they suffer the consequences of disobedience. As *Rashi* and *Ramban* explain the
passage, Moses informed them that *Eretz Yisrael*, which they would soon be entering, was
different from Egypt inasmuch as *Eretz Yisrael's* fertility was dependent directly upon the
bounty of rain from heaven, while Egypt was irrigated regularly by the overflow of the
Nile. *Eretz Yisrael's* rain would be withheld or granted according to Israel's faithfulness to
God, for His special attention is directed to that land, and He gives it rain only if His
Torah is obeyed.

13. וְהָיָה — *And it will come to pass.* In the
verses preceding this one in the Torah
[*Deut.* 11:1-12], Israel is promised a
blessed, prosperous life in *Eretz Yisrael*, a
land "which drinks water of the rain of
heaven" [ibid. *v.* 11]. *Rashi* writes that this
condition is dependent upon our behavior,
and the opening word in passage, וְהָיָה, *and
it will come to pass* [*v.* 13], refers back to
the description in *v.* 11 of *Eretz Yisrael's*
dependence on God for rain, and implies
that the foregoing blessings will be fulfilled
— וְהָיָה, *And it will come to pass* — on the
condition that you hearken to God's
commandments ... for, if you do — [*v.* 14]:
then I will provide rain for your land, etc.

אִם שָׁמֹעַ תִּשְׁמְעוּ אֶל מִצְוֺתַי — *If you
continually hearken* [lit. *if hearken you will
hearken;* in Scriptural style, the compound
infinitive serves to emphasize the verb] *to
My commandments.* [Moses now speaks in
the name of God.]

The use of the compound verb implies
continuity in observance: If you hearken to
what you have already studied you will
hearken to new subjects as well. [As *Me'am
Loez* explains, if someone involves himself
diligently in mastering and remembering
what he has learned, his understanding will
increase and he will inevitably go on to
increase his knowledge. The same holds
true for the performance of commandments — if someone applies himself to them
conscientiously, he will find himself going
on to newer and greater accomplishments.]
Conversely, the idiom אִם שָׁכֹחַ תִּשְׁכַּח, *if
you continually forget* [*Deut.* 8:19] means:
If you have begun to forget, ultimately you

will forget it all. Compare the passage in
Megillas Setarim [some versions read "in
the Megillah," and "Megillas Chassidim";
the exact reference, however, is unknown]:
"If you forsake Me one day, I will forsake
you two days" (*Rashi*).

Yerushalmi Berachos 9:5 illustrates the
last quoted concept as follows: If two
people part from each other — one going
east and the other west, at the end of one
day they will be two days distance from
one another. [Thus, we are enjoined in this
passage of *Shema* to continually hearken to
the *mitzvos;* to neglect them — even for a
short while — results in an unbridgeable
gap.]

אֲשֶׁר אָנֹכִי מְצַוֶּה אֶתְכֶם — *Which I command
you.* They must be fulfilled not because
reason dictates it, but because *I* command
you; *mitzvos* must be performed because
they represent God's will (*Me'am Loez*).

הַיּוֹם — *This day.* That is, as if I commanded
them to you this day. [Thus, though the
Torah was given thousands of years ago,
we should fulfill its precepts as
enthusiastically as if we had received them
only today.] The *mitzvos* should always be
fresh to you as though you heard them
today for the very first time (*Rashi; Sifre*).

Similarly, we must always fulfill the
mitzvos as if their fulfillment were possible
only הַיּוֹם, *that very day,* and if we were to
wait for the morrow we might forfeit the
opportunity. Man must never put off the
performance of a *mitzvah* for the next day
since we are but mortals and cannot be
assured of still being alive tomorrow
(*Divrei Shlomo*).[1]

1. An additional interpretation of this passage is that we must perceive the reward for Torah
observance as being earned on the basis of performing to our capacity, rather than by the *quantitative*
accomplishments we achieve. Thus, if one person does his best *qualitatively* according to his own

One should bear in mind before reciting the next paragraph that he is about to declare his belief in the principle of reward and punishment.

Deuteronomy **13** And it will come to pass — if you continually hearken
11:13-21 to My commandments which I command you this
day, to love HASHEM, your God, and to serve Him, with
all your heart and with all your soul — **14** then I will

לְאַהֲבָה אֶת ה' אֱלֹהֵיכֶם — *To love HASHEM, your God.* Do not perform *mitzvos* for an ulterior motive such as status or profit. Do them out of love for God, and eventually the honor will come *(Rashi).*

וּלְעָבְדוֹ בְּכָל לְבַבְכֶם וּבְכָל נַפְשְׁכֶם — *And to serve him, with all your heart and with all your soul.* The verse commands us to "serve" God with all our "heart." The word serve usually implies a deed. What is "service of the heart"? — service of the heart is prayer *(Taanis 29; Rashi).* Rambam in *Hilchos Tefillah* 1:1 (see *Kessef Mishnah)* and *Semag, Asin* §19 accordingly infer from our passage the requirement to serve God daily with prayer.

While praying one must devote his *total* concentration to God, and allow no stray thought to enter his mind. The Rabbis inferred from this passage that "prayer without concentration [וַכַּוָּנָה] is like a body without a soul" *(Chovos Halevavos Shaar HaNefesh 3).*

Why does the Torah repeat *with all your*

heart and with all your soul when this had already been mentioned in the first portion of *Shema?* — Because that admonition was addressed to the people as individuals [the entire first section of *Shema* is worded in the singular], while this was an admonition addressed [in plural] to the entire community *(Rashi).*

Maskil l'David explains that *Rashi's* differentiation between an individual and a community is intended to explain why this portion — directed to the community — omits the requirement that God be served *with all your resources,* a requirement that *does* appear in the first portion of *Shema.* In the phrase וּבְכָל מְאֹדֶךָ in the first portion, *Rashi* noted that the requirement to love God with all one's resources was mandated to individuals because there are some people whose resources are dearer to them than their own lives [see comm. p. 23.] However, such a perverted idea could not apply to a community as a whole, which could not place greater value to its treasury than its very survival.[1]

ability, but a more gifted person accomplishes more while expending much less effort, the first is more worthy of reward. We must never become frustrated that we cannot possibly achieve *total* fulfillment of the *mitzvos,* nor hope to master the entire realm of Torah knowledge. Our reward comes from our day-to-day effort, as the Sages said [*Pirkei Avos* 2:21]: "It is not up to you to complete the work, yet you are not free to desist from it." The good that God wants to see accomplished on earth is not meant for any *individual* to complete. No one has the right to argue, "what I can do is but so little," and sit back idly. Even if our utmost effort yields only a fraction of what must be accomplished, our reward will be great nevertheless because we have contributed what is expected of us.

The Midrash cites a parable: Someone engaged a group of day laborers to fill a great well with water — a futile task. The fools among them said, "I'll *never* complete this task; it's futile!" But the wise ones among them said, "Look. I'm being paid daily for my labor; what do I care how deep the well is? To the contrary, I should be grateful that it's so deep; I'm assured of a job for a long time!"

The Holy One, Blessed is He, said similarly to mankind, "Study and observe *mitzvos* daily, and you will be paid your reward on that basis. I will not castigate you for not having learnt more than you were able to."

1. One of the disciples of the *Chiddushei HaRim* misused public funds. The rebbe admonished him severely for his conduct, even going so far as to call him a "murderer."

When the rebbe's intimates asked him why he had called this man a "murderer" when he was charged only with robbery, the rebbe answered, "In the second portion of Shema the term מְאֹד, resources, does not appear because that portion is addressed to the community as a whole and public resources are included in the phrase *all your soul.* Such public monies are sanctified for charitable needs, saving lives, supporting widows and orphans — whoever dares tamper with such holy funds may truly be termed a murderer."

מְטַר־אַרְצְכֶם בְּעִתּוֹ יוֹרֶה וּמַלְקוֹשׁ וְאָסַפְתָּ דְגָנֶךָ
טו   וְתִירֹשְׁךָ וְיִצְהָרֶךָ: וְנָתַתִּי עֵשֶׂב בְּשָׂדְךָ לִבְהֶמְתֶּךָ וְאָכַלְתָּ

[For another explanation of why *all your resources* is mentioned only in connection with individuals, see comm. to first section.]

R' Hirsch suggests that מְאֹדְכֶם, *with all your resources*, is not needed in the context of this verse already implied in וּלְעָבְדוֹ, *and to serve him*. The requirement to serve God demands implicitly that one devote all his energies and means to accomplish God's will; if he withholds his resources from this mission, he is limiting his service of God. When our verse speaks of *heart* and *soul*, it refers to the *manner* in which God is to be served — energetically, cheerfully, and unrestrainedly.

14. The reward for compliance

"When you do what you are obligated to do, I, in turn, will do what I am committed to do [and repay your loyalty]" (*Sifre; Rashi*) ...

Here again, Moses speaks in the first-person, as he did in the first verse of this portion, because he speaks in the name of God and apparently cites His words:

וְנָתַתִּי מְטַר אַרְצְכֶם בְּעִתּוֹ — *Then I will provide rain for your land in its proper time.* — So Eretz Yisrael can truly be described as a land "which drinks water of the rain of heaven" [see *Rashi v.* 13].

The blessing of rain is given priority because everything else depends upon precipitation in its proper season: physical health, good harvests, and fruitful cattle (*Rambam* to Levit. 26:4).

Then I will provide — "I" [God], Myself will provide you with these blessings — not through the agency of an angel or emissary (*Sifre*).

Each rainfall will be an act of God's direct Providence, and not *solely* the result of meteorological laws of nature. Although the laws of nature, too, are His creation, the *primary* cause of rain is not predetermined, but remains God's providential care *(R' Hirsch)*.

Rashi — citing *Sifre* — explains that *in its proper time* refers to convenient times, such as nighttime — especially Sabbath eves — when people are usually at home and would not be inconvenienced by rain. [See *Taanis* 23a where Wednesday evening

is also mentioned in this context; cf. *Mizrachi.*]

Rashi is drawn to this Midrashic interpretation rather than the seemingly obvious interpretation that *proper time* refers to the most propitious times for agriculture, since such an advantageous schedule of rainfall is implied in the promise '*I will provide rain for your land.*' If rain were to fall out of season, it would do the land no good and could surely not be considered a blessing. *In its proper time*, therefore, must suggest the deeper connotation that *Rashi* elicits from the Midrash (*Mizrachi*).

The Hebrew term used in our verse for rain, מְטָר, denotes the kind of rain that is a gift of God and a symbol of Divine favor. There is also a 'natural' rain that forms as a result of the vapor ascending to the clouds from the earth. Such rain is called גֶּשֶׁם and comes randomly; it may or may not be propitious (*Malbim* to Gem. 2:5).

יוֹרֶה וּמַלְקוֹשׁ — *The early and late rains.* יוֹרֶה, *early rain*, is rain that falls in Eretz Yisrael in the planting season [Cheshvan — October and November] and drenches [מַרְוֶה] the soil; מַלְקוֹשׁ, *late rain* [from the root לקש which means *late, retarded* [see *Onkelos, Genesis* 30:42]] is the spring showers [in Nissan — March and April] that fall before the harvest and ripen the grain on the stalk (*Rashi; Taanis* 6a).

Another reason for the name יוֹרֶה for *early rain* is given in the Talmud, *Taanis* 6a: These rains [announcing as they do, the impending winter season] 'instruct' [from ירה, *teach*] people to plaster their roofs, to gather in their fruit, and attend to their [winter] needs.

Ibn Ezra similarly explains that יוֹרֶה refers to the *early rains* — since rain in that season *portends* [יוֹרֶה] a propitious year.

According to *Sifre* יוֹרֶה is derived from ירה [arrows] since it falls torrentially, penetrating the soil like an arrow.

Eretz Yisrael's fertility was dependent on the regular start of these periods of rain, especially the first rain. The lack of rain in Cheshvan was regarded as a sign of Divine displeasure and portended great natural calamity. Such droughts would bring about the imposition of public fasts [תַּעֲנִית צִבּוּר] of increasing severity, as recorded in *Taanis* 6a and 15a [see ArtScroll Mishnah, *Taanis* with *Yad Avraham* commentary].

וְאָסַפְתָּ דְגָנֶךָ וְתִירֹשְׁךָ וְיִצְהָרֶךָ — *That you may gather in your grain, your wine, and your oil.* The emphasis is on וְאָסַפְתָּ: *You*, and

provide rain for your land in its proper time, the early and late rains, that you may gather in your grain, your wine, and your oil. [15] I will provide grass in your field for your cattle and you will eat and be satisfied. [16] Beware lest your

not your enemies, will gather in the produce *(Rashi).*

— This and the next verse change to the second-person *singular* to emphasize that each *individual* Jew will benefit from the nation's compliance with God's Torah *(R' Bachya).*

The translation of תִּירֹש as *wine* follows *Onkelos.* Although in the Torah the terms יַיִן and תִּירֹש are synonymous, the *Talmud* notes that in common usage there is a distinction between תִּירֹש, which referred to a sweeter, less fermented wine, and יַיִן which referred to fully aged wine (see *Rashi* to *Nedarim* 76b). Apparently, however, even תִּירֹש would be intoxicating when consumed in sufficient quantity (see *Sanhedrin* 70b).

יִצְהָר [from the root צהר, *light*] refers to pure olive oil used for kindling lamps *(Etz Yosef).*

As noted on p. 63, the *Shema* parallels the Ten Commandments. *Yerushalmi Berachos* 1:5 explains that our verse parallels the commandment: You shall not steal — וְאָסַפְתָּ דְגָנֶךָ, *that you may gather in* your *grain,* and not your neighbor's grain.

Oznaim LaTorah suggests that this is why our verse is in singular. Were it in plural the parallel exegesis prohibiting stealing could not have been elicited.

According to *Acharis Shalom,* the passage is in singular to allude to the fact that crops will be so abundant that each individual will be totally occupied in gathering his own produce.[1]

15. וְנָתַתִּי עֵשֶׂב בְּשָׂדְךָ לִבְהֶמְתֶּךָ [And] *I will provide grass [or: herbage] in your field for your cattle.* The blessing is that you will

find pasturage for your cattle in your own fields, and will not have to lead them a long distance away to graze *(Rashi* from *Sifre).*

In an alternate interpretation from *Sifre, Rashi* explains that the passage means that grain will grow so profusely that one will be able to constantly cut his grain for fodder throughout the rainy season when it grows; and by discontinuing his cutting for a mere thirty days before the harvest, his field will yield as large a crop as if he had not been cutting for the cattle.

וְאָכַלְתָּ וְשָׂבָעְתָּ — *And you will eat and be satisfied.* This refers to *your grain, your wine, and your oil* in the preceding verse *(Ibn Ezra).*

This is a new blessing [not to be understood as being in consequence of God's giving grass in the fields for the cattle. Rather, it is a blessing to man himself.] It implies that a blessing will be on the bread within the stomach, meaning that one will feel sated with what he eats *(Rashi).*

[As *Rashi* comments in *Levit.* 25:19 and 26:35, this blessing means that one need not eat much in order to be full. Rather the idea is that he will find satisfaction in the food he eats. The food itself, as it were, will be blessed (see *Ramban).*]

According to *Ramban,* this phrase modifies the previous phrases: you will eat *your grain, wine, and oil,* as well as the offspring of the thriving cattle, for when *I will provide grass* — *you will be satisfied.*

From the fact that the Torah here speaks *first* of pasture for the cattle, and only *then* continues: *and you will eat and be satisfied,* the Sages deduce that one must first feed his animals before partaking of his own

---

1. In *Berachos* 35b, R' Yishmael understands this verse to mean that despite the Jew's paramount obligation to engage in the study of Torah, he must not rely on miracles for his livelihood. Thus, *You may gather in your grain* is telling us to engage also in work and commerce when necessary. R' Shimon bar Yochai disagrees: 'If a man plows at plowing time, sows at sowing time, harvests at harvest time, threshes at threshing time, and winnows at winnow time, what will become of Torah [study]? Rather, when Jews are *perfectly* righteous, God sees to it that their needs are provided by others; when they are only relatively righteous [see *Tos.* s.v. כאן] they will be forced to see to their own livelihoods.

Abaye observed that those who attempted to follow R' Shimon's course of relying on miracles did not succeed. *Maharsha* explains that R' Shimon never intended his advice except for people with the highest degree of righteousness. For such people, it is indeed more important that they dedicate themselves totally to service of God.

Nevertheless the *Halachah* is clear *(Rambam, Hil. Talmud Torah* 3:6-7; *Yoreh De'ah* 241:1) that the preferred course is that one should give his Torah studies priority to whatever degree possible.

טו וְשָׂבָעְתָּ: הִשָּׁמְרוּ לָכֶם פֶּן־יִפְתֶּה לְבַבְכֶם וְסַרְתֶּם
טז וַעֲבַדְתֶּם אֱלֹהִים אֲחֵרִים וְהִשְׁתַּחֲוִיתֶם לָהֶם: וְחָרָה
אַף־יהוה בָּכֶם וְעָצַר אֶת־הַשָּׁמַיִם וְלֹא־יִהְיֶה מָטָר
וְהָאֲדָמָה לֹא תִתֵּן אֶת־יְבוּלָהּ וַאֲבַדְתֶּם מְהֵרָה מֵעַל
יז הָאָרֶץ הַטֹּבָה אֲשֶׁר יהוה נֹתֵן לָכֶם: וְשַׂמְתֶּם אֶת־דְּבָרַי
אֵלֶּה עַל־לְבַבְכֶם וְעַל־נַפְשְׁכֶם וּקְשַׁרְתֶּם אֹתָם לְאוֹת

meal. [The *halachah*, however, is that this stricture applies only to food. Concerning drink, however, man takes precedence as we derive from *Genesis* 24:14 where Rebecca offers drink to Eliezer before his camels (*Magen Avraham* to *Shulchan Aruch O. Ch.* 167:18. See footnote to ArtScroll *Bereishis ad loc.* p. 911. See also *HaGaon R' Moshe Feinstein, Igros Moshe, Orach Chaim II,* responsa 52).]

16. Warning against violating the Torah

As in *Deut.* 8:11, after the words, *Eat and be satisfied,* a warning note is sounded — *'Beware!'* Satiety induces forgetfulness of God, for prosperity is the greatest challenge to piety.

הִשָּׁמְרוּ לָכֶם פֶּן יִפְתֶּה לְבַבְכֶם — *Beware lest your heart be seduced.* — When you have eaten and are full, beware that you do not rebel against God, for in time of prosperity one needs particularly to be on guard against disloyalty to God, as indicated in *Deut.* 8:12-14, where first it says: *Lest you will have eaten your fill ... and your herds and flocks are multiplied,* and then: *and your heart will grow haughty and you will forget your God* (*Rashi*).

Cf. also *Deut.* 32:15 וַיִּשְׁמַן יְשֻׁרוּן וַיִּבְעָט, *When Jeshurun grew fat, it kicked* (*Dover Shalom*).

Lest your heart be seduced, into attributing the blessings you enjoy to 'other gods' (*Ibn Caspi*).

Chizkuni interprets this verb not as *seduce* — in which case, he suggests, the context would demand the reflexive יִפּוּתֶה — but from the cognate root פתי, foolishness. He renders: *Lest your heart become foolish.*

וְסַרְתֶּם וַעֲבַדְתֶּם אֱלֹהִים אֲחֵרִים וְהִשְׁתַּחֲוִיתֶם לָהֶם — *And you turn astray and serve the gods of others and bow to them. And you turn astray* — from the Torah — *and serve the gods of others,* for if man neglects the Torah he begins a course that will end in idolatry (*Rashi*).

The phrase אֱלֹהִים אֲחֵרִים, literally, *other gods,* [cannot be taken in the sense that there are indeed other Divinities with godly powers. Rather, it] means *gods of others:* they are not gods but others worship them as such. Alternatively, it refers to gods that are 'other' [i.e., alien] to those who worship them; one calls upon them and they do not respond; consequently they became like 'strangers' to him (*Rashi* here and in *Exodus* 20:3).

17. וְחָרָה אַף־ה' בָּכֶם — *Then the wrath of HASHEM will blaze against you.* The expression חָרָה אַף denotes outwardly displayed, flared up anger. The expression is idiomatic and metaphorically refers to *flaring nostrils. Rashi* in *Exodus* 15:8 explains that this term is used to describe *fierce anger* since, when one is angry, the nostrils flare up and become 'hot.' Conversely, when one's anger subsides one is described as נִתְקָרְרָה דַעְתּוֹ, *his mind becomes cooled.*

Of course, when speaking of God, this expression cannot be taken literally since God is incorporeal. Such usage — where physical or emotional attributes are ascribed to God — is termed "anthropomorphism" and "anthropopathism" respectively. "The Torah speaks in the language of men," and such expressions figuratively depict these emotions from the human vantage point.

וְעָצַר אֶת הַשָּׁמַיִם וְלֹא יִהְיֶה מָטָר — *He will restrain the heaven so there will be no rain.* [Rain, as noted, is a gift of God. In times of His wrath, he withholds it.]

This verse is preceded by a reference to idolatry. We derive from this that as a result of the sin of idolatry, rain is withheld (*Yerushalmi, Taanis* 3:3).

וְהָאֲדָמָה לֹא תִתֵּן אֶת יְבוּלָהּ — *And the soil will not yield its produce.* — It will not even yield what you have brought [Hebrew cognate verb מוֹבִיל, from root יבל] to it; your harvest will not even equal the

*heart be seduced and you turn astray and serve the gods
of others and bow to them. 17 Then the wrath of HASHEM
will blaze against you. He will restrain the heaven so there
will be no rain and the soil will not yield its produce. And
you will swiftly be banished from the goodly land which
HASHEM gives you. 18 Place these words of Mine upon
your heart and upon your soul; bind them for a sign upon*

quantity of seed you planted in it. See
Haggai 1:6 (Rashi).
[Comp. *Rashi* on *Leviticus* 26:40: *And
your land will not yield its produce* (וְיבוּלָה):
— Even what you brought (מוֹבִיל) to it at
planting time.]

וַאֲבַדְתֶּם מְהֵרָה מֵעַל הָאָרֶץ הַטֹּבָה — *And you
will swiftly be banished from* [upon] *the
goodly land*. First will come famine. If that
does not bring repentance, exile will follow
(Vilna Gaon).

The word וַאֲבַדְתֶּם, from the root אבד, is
usually rendered *perish*. In this case,
however, *Rashi* — following *Sifre* — maintains that *perishing* from the land is not
what the context implies, nor that death
would be the consequence of the lack of
rain and its attendant famine. [For had אבד
the implication of *perish*, the passage
should have read וַאֲבַדְתֶּם עַל הָאָרֶץ, not מֵעַל הָאָרֶץ
(Torah Temimah).] Rather, the verse now
introduces an *additional* calamity with
which God would punish them — exile
from the land. Furthermore, mention of *the
goodly* land suggests that their sin of
idolatry was due to the abundance of good
which the Land had given them, indicating
that we are not dealing here with a famine.
Instead, this calamity results from a
prosperity that dulls awareness of God; as
Rashi writes above, satiety induces
forgetfulness of God, and as noted above,
the *good land* will provide that satiety.
[*Chizkuni* and *Radak* also interpret this
passage in the sense of exile. (Comp. *Isaiah*
27:13 where הָאוֹבְדִים also means *exiles*).]

Sforno, however, subscribes to the view that
וַאֲבַדְתֶּם is to be interpreted *You shall perish* —
from the famine mentioned in the previous
passage, which will be more severe than death by
the sword.

The meaning of מְהֵרָה, *swiftly* is: You
will be given no probationary period. But,
should you ask, why was the generation of
the Flood granted a 120 year probationary
period before God brought the Flood on

them [see *Rashi* to *Genesis* 6:4]? — The
answer is: The generation of the Flood had
no one from whom to learn, while you *do*
have examples from whom to learn *(Rashi;
Sifre)*.

אֲשֶׁר ה' נֹתֵן לָכֶם — *Which HASHEM gives
you*. I.e., will give you. [Although the land
had not yet been given to Israel, Moses
uses the present tense, *gives*, because God's
assurance to do something is no less real
than a historical fact.]

18. Tefillin, Torah-study, and mezuzah/The observance of mitzvos in Exile

וְשַׂמְתֶּם אֶת־דְּבָרַי אֵלֶּה עַל לְבַבְכֶם וְעַל
נַפְשְׁכֶם — *Place these words of Mine upon
your heart and upon your soul*. It is
contextually unclear why the commandments of *tefillin* and *mezuzah*, mentioned
further in this verse, are reiterated here
after the threat of exile from the Land.
Rashi, following *Sifre* [as explained by
Rambam; see below], interprets that this
verse stresses the necessity for Torah
observance even in Exile [lest one think
that observance of the *mitzvos* applies only
in *Eretz Yisrael*].

In *Rashi's* words: *And place these words
of Mine*, etc.: Even after you have been
exiled, make yourselves distinctive [from
the residents of the gentile nations among
whom you will be dispersed] by means of
My precepts: Don *tefillin*, attach *mezuzos*
to your doorposts, so that they will not be
novelties to you when you return [to *Eretz
Yisrael* where their performance has a
degree of holiness far beyond that
attainable elsewhere *(R' Bachya; see
Ramban* below)]. Similarly, Scripture
records in *Jeremiah* 31:21 [where Jeremiah
addressed the following prophecy to the
Israelites who were about to go into the
Babylonian exile]: *"Set up distinguishing
marks for yourselves"* [that is, retain your
distinctiveness in exile through the
commandments].

יט עַל־יֶדְכֶם וְהָיוּ לְטוֹטָפֹת בֵּין עֵינֵיכֶם: וְלִמַּדְתֶּם אֹתָם
אֶת־בְּנֵיכֶם לְדַבֵּר בָּם בְּשִׁבְתְּךָ בְּבֵיתֶךָ וּבְלֶכְתְּךָ בַדֶּרֶךְ
כ וּבְשָׁכְבְּךָ וּבְקוּמֶךָ: וּכְתַבְתָּם עַל־מְזוּזוֹת בֵּיתֶךָ
כא וּבִשְׁעָרֶיךָ: לְמַעַן יִרְבּוּ יְמֵיכֶם וִימֵי בְנֵיכֶם עַל הָאֲדָמָה

Thus, *Ramban* explains, from the Midrashic expositions cited by *Rashi* — wherein the *mitzvos* of *tefillin*, Torah study, and *mezuzah* are reiterated in this context of exile — we derive that these commandments — and others like them — are personal obligations [חוֹבַת הַגּוּף], in contrast to commandments that apply only to the land [חוֹבַת קַרְקַע]. Personal commandments are binding everywhere, and we are obligated to observe them even in Exile, whereas we are exempt in Exile from commandments which apply to the land (חוֹבַת הַקַּרְקַע) such as heave-offerings and tithes, since land-related commandments apply only in *Eretz Yisrael*. [See *Ramban* to *Leviticus* 18:28 for his elaboration on the qualitative superiority of *mitzvah*-performance in *Eretz Yisrael*. See also R' Nosson Scherman's Overview to *Lech-Lecha* in ArtScroll *Bereishis*.]

Others, such as *Ibn Ezra*, who follow the non-Midrashic sense of the verse, do not perceive this as referring to *mitzvah*-observance in Exile, but as a summary and exhortation of how Israel is to *avoid* the disasters foreboded in the previous verses. They would render: *Thus, you shall place these words of Mine*, etc. — so you will not be exiled — but *prolong your days in your land* (v. 21).

Sforno renders: *Place ... upon your heart* — to meditate thereon; *and upon your soul* — to fulfill them willingly.

◆§ Tefillin

וּקְשַׁרְתֶּם אֹתָם לְאוֹת עַל־יֶדְכֶם — [*And*] *bind them for a sign upon your arm.* [See comm. to parallel phrase in first section, p. 26].

From the continuity in this verse of the word וּקְשַׁרְתֶּם, *bind them*, with the word in the preceding passage, עַל לְבָבְכֶם, *upon your heart*, the Sages in the Talmud [*Menachos* 37b] derive that *tefillin* are to be worn high up on the arm opposite the heart.

The symbolism of the positions of both *tefillin* are clearly stated in the prayer customarily recited daily before *tefillin* are donned: "He has commanded us to lay the *tefillin* on the arm as a memorial of His outstretched arm; and that it should be opposite the heart, to subjugate thereby the desires and designs of our heart to His service, blessed is His Name; and upon the head opposite the brain, so that the soul, which is in my brain, along with my other senses and faculties, may all be subjugated to His service, blessed is His Name.

וְהָיוּ לְטוֹטָפֹת בֵּין עֵינֵיכֶם — *And they shall be* [for] *tefillin between your eyes.* [See comm. to parallel phrase in the First Portion p. 28.]

◆§ Torah-study

וְלִמַּדְתֶּם אֹתָם אֶת־בְּנֵיכֶם — [*And you shall*] *teach them to your children.*[1] Accustom your children to *mitzvos* (*Sforno*).

The word אֹתָם is pronounced אֹתָם, *them*, referring to the words of Torah which you are to teach your children. But it can also be pronounced אַתֶּם, *you*, as if to say וְלִמַּדְתֶּם אַתֶּם, *you are to study* [Torah]. Do not content yourself with making sure your children study. Unless you set a proper *personal* example for them, why should they heed your urgings that *they* study? (*Chofetz Chaim*).[2]

1. The chassidic master, R' Simcha Bunam of P'schis'cha, said of someone who urged his children to study although he studied very little himself: "We can assume that his children will not become scholars, because their father did not set an example. But at least we can be sure that they will urge *their* children to study."

2. In discussing public education of children, the Talmud [*Bava Basra* 21a] records the following:
The name of R' Yehoshua ben Gamla is to be recalled for the good, for were it not for him the Torah would have been forgotten in Israel. At first, if a child had a father, his father taught him, and if he had no father he did not learn at all. They were guided by the verse, *Teach them to your children*, emphasizing that everyone should teach his own children.
They then made an ordinance that teachers be appointed in Jerusalem; in this they were guided by

סדר קריאת שמע [38]

your arm and they shall be tefillin between your eyes.
¹⁹ Teach them to your children, to discuss them while you
sit in your home, while you walk on the way, when you
recline and when you arise. ²⁰ And write them on the
doorposts of your house and upon your gates. ²¹ In order
to prolong your days and the days of your children upon

The Talmud hometically propounds that the word וְלִמַּדְתֶּם [*and you shall teach them*] can be read as if vowelized וְלַמֵּד תַּם [*study perfectly*]. This means that one's study [לִמּוּד] must be enunciated faultlessly [תַּם]. One must make a pause between similar sounds [רֶוַח בֵּין הַדְּבֵקִים]. That is, if the last letter of a word is the same as the first letter of the next, care must be taken not to slur them together, or they will sound like one long word. Examples of such words in the *Shema*, between which one must be careful to pause and enunciate clearly, are: עַל לְבָבֶךָ; עַל לְבַבְכֶם; בְּכָל לְבָבְךָ; בְּכָל לְבַבְכֶם; עֵשֶׂב בְּשָׂדֶךָ; וַאֲבַדְתֶּם מְהֵרָה; הַכָּנָף פְּתִיל; אֶתְכֶם מֵאֶרֶץ (*Berachos* 15b).

לְדַבֵּר בָּם — *To discuss them.* Constantly (*Sforno*) ...

From the time a child can speak, his father should teach him the verse תּוֹרָה צִוָּה לָנוּ מֹשֶׁה מוֹרָשָׁה קְהִלַּת יַעֲקֹב, *Moses commanded us the Torah as a possession of the congregation of Jacob* [*Deut.* 33:4], so that Torah study is the foundation upon which he is taught to speak. Also, the father should accustom the child to the Hebrew language and Torah (*Rashi; Succah* 42a).

בְּשִׁבְתְּךָ בְּבֵיתֶךָ וּבְלֶכְתְּךָ בַדֶּרֶךְ ... — *While you sit in your home,* [*and*] *while you walk on the way.* In giving the command to educate children, the verse speaks in the plural [וְלִמַּדְתֶּם]: this alludes to a communal responsibility to arrange for the education of children. Then it reverts to the singular, *while you sit* [בְּשִׁבְתְּךָ]: this teaches that the individual parent is not absolved from his personal duty to teach his own child (*Iyun Tefillah*).

The verse is homiletically interpreted: *while dwelling at your home* — in *Eretz Yisrael, while walking on the way* — in Exile; *while you recline* — when you are in degraded circumstances *and while you arise* — when you are on the ascendant.

וּכְתַבְתָּם עַל מְזוּזוֹת בֵּיתֶךָ וּבִשְׁעָרֶיךָ — *And write them on the doorposts of your house and upon* [lit. *in*] *your gates.* [See comm. to parallel phrase end of first section.]

[Although many *siddurim* set verse 21 as a new paragraph, leading some to believe that there are *four* paragraphs in the *Shema*, the verse is part of the chapter which begins וְהָיָה and no special separation sets it off in the Torah.]

21. לְמַעַן יִרְבּוּ יְמֵיכֶם וִימֵי בְנֵיכֶם — *In order to prolong your days and the days of your children.* If you fulfill the aforesaid *mitzvos* [*love of God; Torah-study; tefillin; mezuzah*] even in Exile, you will return to *Eretz Yisrael* and enjoy longevity there (following *Rashi* and *Rambam* in v. 18). Alternatively, while you are in *Eretz Yisrael* you should fulfill the aforesaid *mitzvos* properly — and *place these words of Mine upon your heart* — so that it will not become necessary to exile you in the first place (the latter follows *Ibn Ezra*).

This passage is conditional: *If* you will fulfill the Torah *then your days ... will be prolonged,* but if not the opposite will happen (*Rashi; Sifre*).

This verse parallels the Commandment "*Honor your father and your mother so your days will be prolonged ... "*

עַל הָאֲדָמָה — *Upon the ground.* I.e., the life-sustaining sacred soil of *Eretz Yisrael* (*Alshich*) ...

the verse [*Isaiah* 2:3]: *For from Zion shall the Torah go forth.* Even so, however, if a child had a father, the father would take him up to Jerusalem and have him taught there; and if not the child would not go there to learn.

They ordained, therefore, that teachers should be appointed in each province and the boys should enter the schools at the age of sixteen or seventeen. But this was problematic, for if the teacher punished them they used to rebel and leave the school.

Ultimately, R' Yehoshua ben Gamla came and ordained that teachers of *young* children should be appointed in each and every town, and that children should enter school at the age of six or seven.

אֲשֶׁר נִשְׁבַּע יהוה לַאֲבֹתֵיכֶם לָתֵת לָהֶם כִּימֵי הַשָּׁמַיִם עַל־הָאָרֶץ:

Before reciting this last portion of Shema one must have in his mind that he is about to fulfill the commandment of declaring that God took us out of Egypt.

לז-לח וַיֹּאמֶר יהוה אֶל־מֹשֶׁה לֵּאמֹר: דַּבֵּר אֶל־בְּנֵי יִשְׂרָאֵל וְאָמַרְתָּ אֲלֵהֶם וְעָשׂוּ לָהֶם צִיצִת

אֲשֶׁר נִשְׁבַּע ה' לַאֲבֹתֵיכֶם לָתֵת לָהֶם — *That HASHEM has sworn to your ancestors to give [it] to them.* The passage specifies that God has sworn to give it לָהֶם, *to them* — the ancestors — not לָכֶם, *to you.* From this [i.e. the fact that the Land was still to be given to the ancestors who had already long-since died — the implication being that they will resurrect in order to receive the Land], the Midrash derives an allusion to תְּחִיַּת הַמֵּתִים, *Resurrection of the Dead,* in the Torah (*Rashi; Sifre*).

The Doctrine of Resurrection of the Dead, i.e. that following the Messianic Redemption all the dead will be revived to once again lead normal lives [see R' Saadiah Gaon *Emunos V'Deos* ch. 7], is one of the essential beliefs of Judaism, and *Rambam* lists it among the primary tenets of the Faith. This ancient Doctrine finds *explicit* expression in many Scriptural references, such as in Hannah's prayer [*I Samuel* 2:6]: *"HASHEM causes death and gives life, casts down into the grave and raises up";* cf. also *Isaiah* 26:19;

Psalms 16:9; more explicitly, *Daniel* 12:2: *Many of those who sleep in the dusty earth shall awaken, these for everlasting life and these for shame* ... [see ArtScroll commentary there].

All of the above references are from the Books of Scripture known as Prophets and Writings; *Rashi* accordingly cites *Sifre* that our verse provides one of the rare allusions to this Doctrine in the Torah itself.

כִּימֵי הַשָּׁמַיִם עַל הָאָרֶץ — *Like the days of the heaven on the earth.* [The idiom means 'forever,' since the heavens will remain in place as long as the universe endures.] This refers to the quality of life. If you obey the Torah, your transitory life on earth will be as worthwhile as the true, heavenly life (*HaKsav V'HaKabbalah*).

Just as the heaven brings abundance to earth — through the sun, moon, rain, and so on — so your righteous lives will be a source of benefit to everything on earth (*Ksav Sofer*).

◆§ The Third Portion [*Numbers* 15:37-41]

The Talmud [*Berachos* 12b] lists five commandments to be found in this portion: 1). The law of *tzitzis* [v. 38]; 2). Remembrance of the Exodus [v. 41]; 3). The requirement to remember all the commandments and to beware of heresy (see *Maharsha*) [v. 39]; 4). Avoidance of sinful thoughts [v. 39]; 5). Avoidance of idolatrous thoughts [v. 39].

"Why does the section of וְהָיָה אִם שָׁמֹעַ precede that of וַיֹּאמֶר ה'? — Because the former section [dealing as it does with all the *mitzvos*] is applicable to both the day and the night, whereas the latter section [which deals primarily with *tzitzis*] is applicable only to the day" [since the wearing of *tzitzis* is not obligatory at night] (*Berachos* 13a).

Later, the Talmud offers an additional reason for the sequence: The section of שְׁמַע precedes וְהָיָה אִם שָׁמֹעַ, because the former mentions *learning* [וְדִבַּרְתָּ בָּם], *teaching* [וְשִׁנַּנְתָּם לְבָנֶיךָ], and *doing* [the *mitzvos* of love of God, *tefillin* and *mezuzah*]; and the section of וְהָיָה אִם שָׁמֹעַ precedes וַיֹּאמֶר ה' because the former mentions both *teaching* and *doing* whereas the latter mentions *doing* only.

In the Scriptural context: This section is the closing paragraph of *Parshas Sh'lach* which deals primarily with the incident of the Spies. Immediately preceding it is the story of the intentional Sabbath-violator who incurred the death penalty for his transgression.

Purpose of the Mitzvah of Tzitzis. *Ramban* maintains that God commanded the *mitzvah* of *tzitzis* after the incident of the Sabbath violation to emphasize that by means of the *mitzvah* of *tzitzis* the Jews will remember all the commandments, including the Sabbath. [See *Rashi* citing R' Moshe HaDarshan on v. 41.]

According to the *Yalkut*, after the incident of the violation Moses told God that these people had violated the Sabbath because the commandments were still new to them and

the ground that HASHEM has sworn to your ancestors to give them, like the days of the heaven on the earth.

Before reciting this last portion of Shema one must have in his mind that he is about to fulfill the commandment of declaring that God took us out of Egypt.

Numbers
15:37-41 ³⁷ **A**nd HASHEM said to Moses, saying: ³⁸ Speak to the Children of Israel and say to them that they are to

not sufficiently ingrained in their minds. During the weekdays, the Jews have a physical 'sign' — *tefillin* — to remind them of the *mitzvos* and the covenant with God that distinguish them from the gentiles; on Sabbath, however, there is no special distinctive symbol. In response God mandated that *tzitzis* be worn — even on the Sabbath — to serve as a *constant* reminder of all the commandments.

The Midrash observes that every moment and activity in a Jew's life is charged and regulated with some sort of commandment. Even when he wraps himself in a garment, God legislated that it be fringed with *tzitzis*.

Furthermore, the Sages invested the precept of *tzitzis* with exalted symbolism. *Tzitzis* is regarded as a reminder to the Jew to observe the *mitzvos*, its function being similar to that of the *mezuzah* on the doorposts and to the *tefillin* on the arm and head. The Talmud [*Menachos* 44a] tells of a person who was saved from sensual sin because he wore *tzitzis*.

Its inclusion in the Shema. The reason this portion was designated as part of the twice-daily recitation of *Shema* is because it recalls the Exodus from Egypt, an event that a Jew is commanded to remember *all the days of your life* [see *Deut.* 16:3]. 'All' is an inclusive word implying something in addition to whatever is stated explicitly. The Sages expound that it teaches the additional obligation to recall the Exodus in the evening as well as the morning.

Although other portions of the Torah mention the Exodus, only this one was selected for inclusion in the *Shema* because, as noted above, it contains a total of five commandments, not only mention of the Exodus (*Berachos* 12b).

According to Talmud *Yerushalmi*, this section was chosen for inclusion in the daily recital of the *Shema* because of its parallel references to the Ten Commandments [see *Tosafos, Berachos* 12b, s.v. בקשו: see also p. 63].

37. וַיֹּאמֶר ה' אֶל מֹשֶׁה לֵּאמֹר — *And HASHEM said to Moses, saying.*[1] The superfluous expression *saying* — literally *to say* — throughout the Torah has the connotation of *to say*, i.e. transmit, to all future generations (לֵאמֹר לְדוֹרוֹת); it also implies that the statement it introduces was transmitted in a clear unambiguous manner. In the case of the transmission of a *mitzvah*, as in our passage, the word *to say* connotes that the relatively brief recorded text was accompanied by elaboration and specifications of the meaning and perfor-

mance of the *mitzvah* in תּוֹרָה שֶׁבְּעַל פֶּה, Oral Law transmitted to Moses at Sinai, and then handed down from generation to generation (*HaKsav V'Hakabbalah*; see *Ramban* beginning of *Leviticus*; *Iyun Tefillah*).

38. דַּבֵּר אֶל בְּנֵי יִשְׂרָאֵל וְאָמַרְתָּ אֲלֵהֶם — *Speak to the Children* [lit. *sons*] *of Israel and say to them.* There is a rule in Biblical interpretation that wherever both terms דַּבֵּר, *speak*, and וְאָמַרְתָּ, *say*, occur in one passage, the former term means: *introduce*

1. The expression וַיֹּאמֶר ה', *HASHEM said*, has a more conciliatory connotation than the common וַיְדַבֵּר ה', *HASHEM spoke*. This reflects the Midrashic interpretation [mentioned in the prefatory comment above] that following the incident of the Sabbath violation recorded in the Torah immediately preceding this verse, Moses was distressed and said to God, "During the weekdays the Jews wear *tefillin* and remember the commandments; what shall they wear on Sabbath to serve as a reminder?"

"I will command them to wear *tzitzis* [which shall apply even on the Sabbath]," God answered, "and this shall remind them of the commandments always." Thus, since God wished to conciliate Moses and respond to his wishes, the term וַיֹּאמֶר is used to introduce this *mitzvah* (*Or HaChaim*).

According to *Harav Moshe Feinstein* שליט"א, the more conciliatory term אמר is used to introduce this *mitzvah*, because *tzitzis* are not obligatory in the same absolute sense as are other *mitzvos*. According to the Scriptural *halachah*, only when one wears a four-cornered garment does the

לט עַל־כַּנְפֵי בִגְדֵיהֶם לְדֹרֹתָם וְנָתְנוּ עַל־צִיצִת הַכָּנָף פְּתִיל תְּכֵלֶת: וְהָיָה לָכֶם לְצִיצִת וּרְאִיתֶם אֹתוֹ וּזְכַרְתֶּם אֶת־

the topic in general, and the latter means: *elaborate upon it*. In the context of this *mitzvah*, this elaboration consists of the number of threads, the manner of tying the knots, etc., all of which are not specified in the Torah, but which we know from the tradition handed down generation to generation from Moses at Sinai. Thus, only the general outline of the mitzvah was recorded in the Torah, but detailed laws, which Moses taught to Israel, remained as the Oral Law (*R' Bachya; Etz Yosef*).

The Rabbis [*Pesikta Zutresa*, see *Hagahos Maimonis*] derive from the specification בְּנֵי יִשְׂרָאֵל, lit. the *'sons' of Israel*, that women are exempt from this commandment; see below, p. 45. Cf. *Tosafos Gittin* §5b and *Torah Temimah* §106.

Furthermore, in the Talmud [*Menachos* 42a], from the phrase *Children of Israel* the law is codified that only a Jew can make *tzitzis*; if a gentile makes *tzitzis* for a Jew they are invalid.

וְעָשׂוּ לָהֶם צִיצִת — *That they are to* [lit. *and they shall*] *make themselves* [lit. *to them*] *tassels.* [Hebrew: *tzitzis*.] *Rashi* offers two reasons why these tassels are called *tzitzis*: a) because of the threads that hang down from it, the term צִיצַת meaning *curls* or *locks*, as in Ezekiel 7:3; b) because the command associated with them is that: *You shall look upon it* [v. 39], and the word צִיצָה, according to this interpretation, is derived from the verb צִיץ, *gaze*, as in *Song of Songs* 2:9, and the noun denotes "an object to be gazed at."

⊷§ Not an absolute command

This verse is not an absolute command, for as noted below, the Torah obligates one to attach *tzitzis* only if he is wearing a four-cornered garment. Rather, the command is conditional, as if to say: If you own a four-cornered garment and wish to wear it, then be aware that you must *first make yourselves tassels* (*HaKsav V'Hakabalah*).

According to accepted *halachah*, *tzitzis* is a חוֹבַת גַּבְרָא, *incumbent on the person*, and not חוֹבַת טַלִּית, *incumbent on the garment*.

That is, the duty is only incumbent when a four-cornered garment is worn, but כְּלִי מוּנָח בְּקוּפְסָא, *a garment in the closet*, need not have *tzitzis*.

As *R' Hirsch* emphasizes in this connection, though the Torah does not require a four-cornered garment be worn, the Torah assumes that we will wear such a garment and expects us to impose this duty on ourselves, as indeed we do. See below.

From the emphasis on the word וְעָשׂוּ, *they are to make*, the Rabbis expound the Law that the *tzitzis* must be specially made for the purpose. The threads used for *tzitzis* must be spun with the expressed intention that they are being made for *tzitzis*. ... Furthermore, previously wound and tied *tzitzis* that are later sewn onto a garment are not valid (*Rambam* 1:11-12; see *Menachos* 42a-b).

Additionally, the superfluous word לָהֶם, *to them*, is interpreted to denote that the *tzitzis* must be of material that belongs to the owner; if one steals thread and makes *tzitzis* from it, it is invalid (*Succah* 9a; *Orach Chaim* 1:6).

עַל כַּנְפֵי בִגְדֵיהֶם לְדֹרֹתָם — *On the corners of their garments, throughout their generations.* Technically the obligation of this *mitzvah* applies only if one is wearing a garment of four or more corners, in which case he must affix *tzitzis* to each of them [*Menachos* 43b; *Orach Chaim* §17 and §24]. When such four-cornered garments, such as four-cornered cloaks, went out of style, a typical wardrobe no longer included a garment that required *tzitzis* [see *Orach Chaim* 10:18]. Then the Rabbis exegetically extended the *mitzvah* and ruled that one *should* wear a four-cornered garment in order to make it possible to fulfill the *mitzvah* לְדֹרֹתָם, *throughout all generations.* [See *Sefer HaChinuch*.]

Accordingly, the *mitzvah* is now fulfilled by means of a *tallis katan* ['small tallis'] or *arba kanfos* ['four corners'] — a rectangular four-cornered undergarment (for adults about 18-24 inches wide by about four feet long; for children,

obligation to attach *tzitzis* to each of the corners apply, but it is only by Rabbinic mandate that one *must* wear such a garment in order to affix *tzitzis* to it. [See *comm.* to *v.* 38 s.v. וְעָשׂוּ] (*R' A. Fishelis, Kol Ram*).

make themselves tassels on the corners of their garments,
throughout their generations. And they are to place upon
the tassels of each corner a thread of t'cheiles. [39] *And it*
shall constitute tassels for you, that you may see it and

proportionately smaller) — with an aperture in the center to let it pass over the head — which is worn all day. In addition, a full-sized *tallis* is worn during morning prayers. To the four corners of such garments are fashioned the *tzitzis*. As is the case with other *mitzvos*, the donning of such garments requires an appropriate benediction. [See *Orach Chaim* 88.]

The word לְדֹרֹתָם, *throughout their generations*, emphasizes that the precept of *tzitzis* — which serves as a remembrance of all the *mitzvos* — applies to *all* generations, even to a wholly righteous one which might think it does not require such symbolic reminders and might think itself exempt from this commandment *(Or HaChaim)*.

Or HaChaim observes further that the word לְדֹרֹתָם, *throughout their generations*, occurs after the command of the *white* threads, not of the *t'cheiles* threads, because in effect only the white threads would be in use for all generations, not the *t'cheiles* [see below]. *(Chasam Sofer* comments similarly.)

From the expression 'on the corners,' the Talmud [*Menachos* 42a] derives that the *tzitzis* must be inserted some distance — at least three finger-breadths — from the corner so that they can *hang* over the corners. It is invalid if the *tzitzis* were attached at the actual corners. This follows · the halachic pratice codified in *Shulchan Aruch*.

The commentators stress that in order to properly fulfill this aspect of the *mitzvah*, the *tzitzis* should be affixed so they are knotted across the vertical part of the garment, so the *tzitzis* will hang *on* the corners, which would not be the case if they were knotted so they hang straight down. [See *Torah Temimah; Shulchan Aruch* 11:15.]

The word כָּנָף, *corner*, also means *wing*. Homiletically, therefore, the wearing of *tzitzis* on the *corners* of garments is a reminder of how God redeemed the Israelites from Egypt "bearing them on eagle's wings" [*Exodus* 19:4] *(Rashi v.* 41 citing *R' Moshe HaDarshan).*

וְנָתְנוּ עַל צִיצִת הַכָּנָף פְּתִיל תְּכֵלֶת — *And they*

are to place upon the tassels of each [lit. of the] *corner a thread* [lit. *a twist* (see *Rashi* to *Deut.* 32:5)] of t'cheiles.

That is, **among** the tassels of each corner there is to be entwined a single thread of *t'cheiles*. In this context, עַל, *upon*, denotes *with*, as in *Levit.* 25:31 עַל שְׂדֵה הָאָרֶץ with *the fields of the country (Chizkuni).*

◄§ T'cheiles

T'cheiles refers to wool died with the bluish color of a rare species of fish known as the *chilazon* (see *Rashi* here and to *Exodus* 25:4).

The exact identity of the *chilazon* is unknown. It is assumed to be a boneless invertebrate, of the snail family, which was so rare that it surfaced but once in seventy years [*Menachos* 44a; see *Rashi* in *Sanhedrin* 91a and *Megillah* 6a]. According to *Megillah* 6a, the *chilazon* was found in the waters of the territory of Zebulun, whose descendants engaged in its traffic [see *Rashi* to *Genesis* 49:34 (ArtScroll ed. p. 2158)].

The color of *t'cheiles* itself is the subject of various opinions, ranging from sky-blue *(Rambam)* to the color of the nighttime sky *(R' Moshe HaDarshan* cited by *Rashi* to *Numbers* 15:41) to a greenish-blue *(Rashi* to our verse [and *Ibn Ezra* to *Exodus* 25:4] who renders יָרֹק. It is not clear if *Rashi* means 'greenish' blue, i.e. aquamarine, but the Talmud compares the color of *t'cheiles* to the sea; see below).

Rambam [Hil. *Tzitzis* 2:1] writes that wherever *t'cheiles* thread is mentioned in the Torah, it refers to wool dyed blue [azure], the color of the clear bright sky. The color must retain its luster and be resistant to fading. [See *Rambam* there for a description of the process by which the blue threads were dyed.]

As noted, even in Talmudic times it was scarce. For many centuries, the identity of the *chilazon* has been unknown. Therefore our *tzitzis* do not contain the *t'cheiles* thread.

Nevertheless, the *mitzvah* of *tzitzis* — i.e. the white threads without the addition of the *t'cheiles* threads — remains binding

כָּל־מִצְוֹת יהוה וַעֲשִׂיתֶם אֹתָם וְלֹא תָתוּרוּ אַחֲרֵי
לְבַבְכֶם וְאַחֲרֵי עֵינֵיכֶם אֲשֶׁר־אַתֶּם זֹנִים אַחֲרֵיהֶם:
מ לְמַעַן תִּזְכְּרוּ וַעֲשִׂיתֶם אֶת־כָּל־מִצְוֹתָי וִהְיִיתֶם קְדֹשִׁים

even in the absence of *t'cheiles* (*Menachos* 38a). [See *Or HaChaim* cited above on לְדֹרֹתָם.]

The number of *t'cheiles* strands, and the manner in which the *t'cheiles* was wrapped and knotted with the white strands are also the subject of controversy among the Talmudic commentators and halachic codifiers [see *Rashi* and *Tosafos*, *Menachos* 38a]. For a description of the knotting and winding with the *t'cheiles* see *Rambam* 1:6-7, and R' G. Ch. Leiner (the 'Radziner'): *Psil T'cheiles* in *S'funei T'munei Chol* p. 113ff.

⏀§ **Manner of Knotting**

Nowadays, when only white threads are used, each tassel consists of one very long and three shorter white threads which are passed through the holes in the four corners of the garment and folded so as to make eight strands. They are then fastened with a double knot. The long thread, known as the *shamash* [lit. *attendant*], is wound around the other threads 7, 8, 11, and 13 times respectively [the total, 39, being the numerical equivalent of ה' אחד, *HASHEM is One* (cf. *Bais Yosef* §11)]. After each prescribed number of windings, a double knot is tied. Each tassel, therefore, will consist of a knot, 7 turns, a knot, 8 turns, a knot, 11 turns, a knot, 13 turns, a knot, and 8 free-hanging threads. Thus, each *tzitzis* consists of 13 elements — 5 double knots and 8 threads (see *Rashi* below s.v. וּרְאִיתֶם).

R' *Hirsch* notes that as fringes of the garment [צִיצַת הַכָּנָף] they are presumed to be מִין כָּנָף, similar to the garment in color. Since garments were predominantly white, *tzitzis* are referred to in general terms as לָבָן, 'white.' But the color is entirely immaterial; they are called white only in the sense that they are not *t'cheiles* (*Menachos* 38a). *Rambam* interprets similarly.

39. וְהָיָה לָכֶם לְצִיצִת — *And it shall constitute tassels for you.* According to *Rashba* [following the second view in *Rashi* on the word צִיצִת]: 'It shall constitute *an object of gazing* for you.'

— The singular [וְהָיָה, *and it shall* constitute, and צִיצִת (the plural would be צִיצִיּוֹת)] indicates that collectively, the white and *t'cheiles* threads together constitute the single *mitzvah* of *tzitzis*. Furthermore, since the fulfillment of the *mitzvah* requires the presence of all *four* tassels — the tying of only three tassels is not even a partial *mitzvah* in the absence of the fourth — all four constitute together the one *mitzvah* of *tzitzis*, rather than four separate *mitzvos* (*Menachos* 28a; *Rambam Hilchos Tzitzis* 1:5).

וּרְאִיתֶם אֹתוֹ וּזְכַרְתֶּם ... וַעֲשִׂיתֶם אֹתָם — *That you may* [lit. *and you shall*] *see it* [i.e. the *tzitzis*, all four, as noted, being considered one *mitzvah* or: according to *Rambam*: that you may see the *t'cheiles*] *and remember all the commandments of HASHEM and perform them.*

The phrase *and you shall see it* indicates that the *tzitzis* must be visible (*Ibn Ezra*).

[This is one of the sources of the custom to wear the *tzitzis* visibly outside of one's garments. However, the simple connotation of *Ibn Ezra's* comment is that the *mitzvah* of *tzitzis* applies only to daytime. See below.]

While reciting these words in the morning, one should hold the lower portion of the *tzitzis* in his right hand while still grasping the higher, knotted, part of the *tzitzis* in his left hand, look at them, and then pass them over his eyes. Customs vary, but many kiss the *tzitzis* as mentioned, in order to display a love for the *mitzvah* (see *Beis Yosef* and *Orach Chaim* 24:5).

The Sages and commentators variously interpret exactly how the *tzitzis* would invoke this 'remembrance' of all HASHEM's *mitzvos*.

Rashi cites *Tanchuma* that the word *tzitzis* [spelled 'full' with both *yuds* as it is pronounced (see *Ramban*; *Daas Zekeinim*; *Mizrachi*; *Gur Aryeh*)] has a numerical value of 600 [צ=90; י=10; צ=90; י=10; ת=400], and each corner contains 13 elements, i.e., 5 knots and 8 threads for a total of 613 — the number of Scriptural commandments. [Thus, as the Sages remarked שְׁקוּלָה צִיצַת כְּנֶגֶד כָּל הַמִּצְוֹת,

remember all the commandments of HASHEM and perform them; and not explore after your heart and after your eyes after which you go astray. ⁴⁰ So that you may remember and perform all My commandments; then you

The *mitzvah* of *tzitzis* is equal to all the other *mitzvos*."]

According to *Ramban*, it is the *t'cheiles* strand that will invoke this recollection of the sum total of the *mitzvos*. For, as the Talmud notes [*Menachos* 43b], *t'cheiles* is reminiscent of the sea, which is reminiscent of the sky, which is reminiscent of God's Throne of Glory which, as noted in *Ezekiel* 1:26, had the appearance of a sapphire stone. Hence, the sight of the *tzitzis* serves as a reminder of one's duties to God. [*Ramban* also records a Kabbalistic reason for the remembrance invoked by the *t'cheiles*.]

The Talmud [*Menachos* 43b] also mentions that *tzitzis* are like an insignia that identifies one as the King's servant, and reminds him of his obligation to loyally abide by the King's commands. For in effect, one should not rely on remembrance alone; man requires something tangible with which to stimulate the remembrance and observance. As the Sages observed, "Seeing leads to remembering, and remembering leads to performance."

The emphasis is on וַעֲשִׂיתֶם אֹתָם, *perform them*, since to remember without action is a useless intellectual exercise *(R' Nosson Scherman)*.

⋖§ Several laws are derived from the expression וּרְאִיתֶם אֹתוֹ, and you shall see it. A sampling:

□ **Women are exempt; blind men are obligated**

The phrase *you shall see it* intimates that the *mitzvah* applies to daytime only which is the "time for seeing" [שְׁעַת רְאִיָּה]. Thus, since *tzitzis* is a מִצְוַת עֲשֵׂה שֶׁהַזְּמַן גְּרָמָא, "a positive precept dependent on a fixed time," women are exempt from it, for women are exempt from time-related precepts *(Rambam, Hil. Tzitzis* 3:7; see *Menachos* 43a; *Shulchan Aruch* 17:1).

Although *seeing* is crucial to this *mitzvah*, four-cornered garments worn by a blind man must have *tzitzis*. The 'seeing' referred to in our verse merely designates daytime as the time of seeing in general, even if a particular individual is deprived

of his sight (see *Menachos* 43a).

□ **The time for reading Shema**

From the phrase *you shall see it*, the Sages derive the time when it is permitted to begin reading the *Shema* in the morning. Since the portion of *tzitzis* is read with *Shema*, it may be presumed that both begin at the same time. The Sages [in *Berachos* 9a] accordingly expound that one may recite the *Shema* in the morning from the time that there is enough daylight to distinguish between *t'cheiles* and white, i.e. the various threads of the *tzitzis* (*Menachos* 43a; cf. *Yerushalmi Berachos* 1:2).

□ **Seeing the Divine Presence**

Homiletically, the word אֹתוֹ is perceived by analogy from *Deut.* 6:13 to refer to God, and our passage accordingly implies that by virtue of the merit of scrupulous observance of the mitzvah of *tzitzis* one becomes worthy of וּרְאִיתֶם אֹתוֹ, 'seeing Him,' i.e., receiving the Divine Presence (*Menachos* 43b).

וְלֹא תָתוּרוּ אַחֲרֵי לְבַבְכֶם וְאַחֲרֵי עֵינֵיכֶם — *And not explore after your heart and after your eyes*. The heart and the eyes are 'spies' for the body, its agents of sin — the eye sees, then the heart craves, then the body sins *(Rashi)*.

The 'heart' [the Biblical metaphor representing the intellect] leads one to heretical thoughts, while one's 'eyes' lead him to crave immorality *(Berachos* 12b).

As noted on p. 63 the passages of *Shema* contain allusions to the Ten Commandments. Our passage parallels the Commandment לֹא תִנְאָף, *You shall not commit adultery*.

אֲשֶׁר־אַתֶּם זֹנִים אַחֲרֵיהֶם — *After which you go astray*. 'Going astray' is an allusion to leaving God's service in favor of idols [see וַיִּזְנוּ in *Judges* 8:33] (*Berachos* 12b).

40. לְמַעַן תִּזְכְּרוּ וַעֲשִׂיתֶם אֶת־כָּל־מִצְוֹתָי — *So that you may remember and perform all My commandments*. The previous verse spoke of remembering God and His commandments, which would be evoked by looking at the *tzitzis*. But this verse informs us that the ultimate *purpose* of this

מא לֵאלֹהֵיכֶם: אֲנִי יהוה אֱלֹהֵיכֶם אֲשֶׁר הוֹצֵאתִי אֶתְכֶם
מֵאֶרֶץ מִצְרַיִם לִהְיוֹת לָכֶם לֵאלֹהִים אֲנִי יהוה
אֱלֹהֵיכֶם: אֱמֶת:

is to reach the point where we do not need external reminders, but that we *ourselves* keep God's commandments constantly in mind and fulfill them *(R' Hirsch)*.

According to the Talmudic opinion noted on p. 63 that passages of *Shema* contain allusions to the Ten Commandments, our passage parallels the Command, זָכוֹר אֶת יוֹם הַשַּׁבָּת, *Remember the Sabbath day.* The Sabbath is equal in importance to all the *mitzvos* of the Torah just as *tzitzis* remind us of all the *mitzvos* (Yerushalmi *Berachos* 1:5).

Shulchan Aruch cautions that while reciting the *Shema*, one be particularly careful to enunciate the ז of תִּזְכְּרוּ, *you may remember,* so it not sound like תִּשְׂכְּרוּ, *you may hire,* or תִּשְׁקְרוּ, *you may falsify.* Similarly, we should enunciate carefully the ז in וּזְכַרְתֶּם.

וִהְיִיתֶם קְדֹשִׁים לֵאלֹהֵיכֶם — *Then you will be holy to your God.* [I.e., as a result of remembering and performing all God's *mitzvos*, you will rise up to a level of being 'holy' to God.]

קָדֹשׁ, *holy,* in its most literal sense, denotes dedication to a specific noble purpose (R' Hirsch).

According to *Rashi* in *Leviticus* 30:2 [following the dictum in *Yerushalmi Yevamos* 2:4] the term 'holy' applies to one who abstains from illicit sexual relationships [an absolution that is fostered by the proper observance of *tzitzis*. The Talmud records several instances where people were saved at the last moment from illicit unions by the sight of their *tzitzis*]. *Rashi* notes that wherever the Torah gives a warning to guard against immorality, it mentions 'holiness' in that context.

Ramban there, however, bases himself on other sources and maintains that the concept of 'holiness' has a more general

application. It intimates practicing temperance and moderation even in permissible matters, such as eating, playing, and enjoying. The Torah does not forbid such pleasures, but the 'holy' person does not indulge himself to the point of becoming gluttonously addicted to such activites. If he oversteps the bounds of moderation such a person could become a נָבָל בִּרְשׁוּת הַתּוֹרָה, *a sordid person with the Torah's* [technical] *permission.* God therefore cautions us to be 'holy' — i.e. to avoid excesses and practice moderation.

41. אֲנִי ה' אֱלֹהֵיכֶם — *I am HASHEM, your God.* [As noted in the *comm.* to the first verse of *Shema*, HASHEM denotes God in His Aspect as Dispenser of Mercy, while *Elohim* [God] describes His Aspect as Dispenser of Justice.]

Rashi accordingly perceives the contextual implication of our passage to be: *I am HASHEM* — faithful to dispense reward [for your compliance]; *your God* — certain to mete out punishment [for violation of the commandments]. No act goes unnoticed.

אֲשֶׁר הוֹצֵאתִי אֶתְכֶם מֵאֶרֶץ מִצְרַיִם לִהְיוֹת לָכֶם לֵאלֹהִים — *Who has removed you from the land of Egypt to be a God to you.* It was for that reason that I removed you from Egypt — that you accept My decrees [i.e., that I be your God] *(Rashi).*

By redeeming the Jews from Egyptian slavery, God placed them under His special Providential care. Their continued existence is thus guaranteed by God *(Sforno).*

While reciting this passage of the *Shema* one should intend to fulfill the *mitzvah* of

will be holy to your God. ⁴¹ *I am HASHEM, your God,*
Who has removed you from the land of Egypt to be a God
to you. I am HASHEM your God. True.

remembering the Exodus from Egypt
(*Arizal*).

Why is the Exodus from Egypt mentioned in
connection with the *tzitzis?* — It intimates: "Just
as in Egypt I distinguished between one who was
genuinely a firstborn and one who was not, I will
also seek out and punish one who deceitfully
attaches a blue-dyed woolen thread to his
garment and pretends it is genuine *t'cheiles"*
(*Rashi; Bava Metzia* 61b).

אֲנִי ה' אֱלֹהֵיכֶם — ... — *I am HASHEM your*
God ... Why is this phrase repeated from
above? — The earlier phrase implied, as
noted above, that God will reward
compliance and punish violation, which
might be construed erroneously to imply
that one might choose never to accept
God's sovereignty upon himself and
thereby avoid reward or punishment. To
negate this, God now reiterated it in
absolute terms: My sovereignty is based
not upon your compliance or acceptance of
Me, but rather, *I am HASHEM your God —*
even against your will. [Comp. *Ezekiel*
20:23] (*Rashi* based on *Sifre;* cf. *Menachos*
44a; *Mizrachi; Be'er Yitzchak; Yalkut*
Yehudah; Sforno; see also *Shabbos* 88a).

Kabbalistically, the repetition implies
that HASHEM is our God in This World
and in the Future World; or just as He
manifested Himself as our God during the
Egyptian Exodus, so will He do at the final
Redemption when He gathers in the Exiles
(*R' Bachya; Sifre*).

⦿§ אֱמֶת — **True.** The word אֱמֶת, which is
the beginning word of the next paragraph
of prayers in the *Siddur*, does not occur in
the Torah, and it is not said when chanting

this portion in the Torah. It is appended to
the recitation of the *Shema* to complete the
total number of 248 words, including the
prefatory formula אֵל מֶלֶךְ נֶאֱמָן, or the three
word repetition of ה' אֱלֹהֵיכֶם אֱמֶת by the
chazzan. [See prefatory *comm.* and *comm.*
to אֵל מֶלֶךְ נֶאֱמָן]. It is read as a three word
declaraton ה', אֱלֹהֵיכֶם אֱמֶת, *HASHEM your*
God, is true. The law of not interrupting
between the last words of *Shema* and אֱמֶת,
true, is of ancient origin and its reason, as
stated in the Talmud [*Berachos* 14a], is so
that we may declare, as did the prophet
[*Jeremiah* 10:10]: וַה' אֱלֹהִים אֱמֶת.

It would seem from this Talmudic law
that the phrase is considered like one verse
of *Shema* which one might not fragmentize
with interruptions. It is curious, however,
why if the law is so well rooted, the word
אֱמֶת does not appear in the Torah at the
end of this verse?

Presumably, it would appear that there
was a tradition known by our Sages
through the Oral Law that the word אֱמֶת
was to have been included in the Torah in
this verse — as it is included in Jeremiah's
prophecy. However, it was omitted because
the very next verse in the Torah [*Numbers*
15:1] introduces the revolt of Korach, and
it is well-known that אֱמֶת, *truth,* is stifled
by controversy. Thus, the word is not
written in the Torah in this place, but may
be said to "hover in the air." The Sages,
however, introduced its recital during the
Shema reading, and it has the force of a
verse in which one may not make
interruptions (*R' Mordechai Y. L. Zaks*
cited in *Itturei Torah* and *Sefer Haparshi-*
yos).

רִבּוֹנוֹ שֶׁל עוֹלָם, הֲרֵינִי מוֹחֵל לְכָל־מִי שֶׁהִכְעִיס וְהִקְנִיט אוֹתִי,
אוֹ שֶׁחָטָא כְנֶגְדִּי — בֵּין בְּגוּפִי, בֵּין בְּמָמוֹנִי, בֵּין
בִּכְבוֹדִי, בֵּין בְּכָל־אֲשֶׁר לִי, בֵּין בְּאָנֶס, בֵּין בְּרָצוֹן, בֵּין בְּשׁוֹגֵג, בֵּין בְּמֵזִיד;
בֵּין בְּדִבּוּר, בֵּין בְּמַעֲשֶׂה, בֵּין בְּמַחֲשָׁבָה, בֵּין בְּהִרְהוּר; בֵּין בְּגִלְגּוּל זֶה, בֵּין
בְּגִלְגּוּל אַחֵר — לְכָל־בַּר יִשְׂרָאֵל, וְלֹא יֵעָנֵשׁ שׁוּם אָדָם בִּסְבָתִי. יְהִי
רָצוֹן מִלְּפָנֶיךָ יהוה אֱלֹהַי וֵאלֹהֵי אֲבוֹתַי, שֶׁלֹּא אֶחֱטָא עוֹד (וְלֹא אֶחֱזוֹר
בָּהֶם, וְלֹא אָשׁוּב עוֹד לְהַכְעִיסֶךָ, וְלֹא אֶעֱשֶׂה הָרַע בְּעֵינֶיךָ). וּמַה־
שֶּׁחָטָאתִי לְפָנֶיךָ מְחוֹק בְּרַחֲמֶיךָ הָרַבִּים, אֲבָל לֹא עַל־יְדֵי יִסּוּרִים
וָחֳלָיִים רָעִים. יִהְיוּ לְרָצוֹן אִמְרֵי־פִי וְהֶגְיוֹן לִבִּי לְפָנֶיךָ, יהוה צוּרִי
וְגוֹאֲלִי.

בָּרוּךְ אַתָּה יהוה אֱלֹהֵינוּ, מֶלֶךְ הָעוֹלָם, הַמַּפִּיל חֶבְלֵי שֵׁנָה
עַל־עֵינַי, וּתְנוּמָה עַל־עַפְעַפָּי (וּמֵאִיר לְאִישׁוֹן בַּת־
עָיִן). וִיהִי רָצוֹן מִלְּפָנֶיךָ יהוה אֱלֹהַי וֵאלֹהֵי אֲבוֹתַי,
שֶׁתַּשְׁכִּיבֵנִי לְשָׁלוֹם וְתַעֲמִידֵנִי (לְחַיִּים טוֹבִים וּ)לְשָׁלוֹם. (וְתֵן

‏‎ קריאת שמע על המטה / The Bedtime Shema

The recital of the *Shema* immediately before retiring is perceived as a שְׁמִירָה, protection, against the dangers of the night (*Shulchan Aruch; Shelah; Zohar*).

"R' Yehoshua ben Levi says: Though one has recited the *Shema* in the synagogue [in the *Maariv* service] it is a *mitzvah* to recite it again upon his bed" (*Berachos* 4b).

R' Yitzchak observed: If one recites the *Shema* upon his bed, it is as though he held a two-edged sword in his hand [to protect him against the evils of the night] ... we derive this from *Psalms* 149:5-6: *Let the righteous exult in glory, let them sing for joy upon their beds*, and then it is written: *Let the praises of God be in their mouth, and a two-edged sword in their hand* (*Berachos* 5a).

The essence of this *Shema* is the *HaMapil* benediction and the first section of *Shema*. The recital of the other psalms and verses are of ancient origin — many of the sources can be traced to the Talmud and earliest halachic treatises [such as *Kol Bo*] (*Eliyah Rabbah*).

Women, too, have the custom of being scrupulous to recite the *Shema* before retiring, because of the protective benefits it offers (*ibid.; Pri Megadim*).

‏‎§ **Prefatory supplication: forgiveness of others and prayer for God's forgiveness and protection**

Before retiring for the evening it is proper for one to examine his deeds of that day; should one discover an ill-deed he should pray for forgiveness and undertake to correct his ways. It is also proper for one to forgive those who wronged him. In merit of this one will attain long life (*Mishnah Berurah* 239:1:9).

Accordingly, many recite this prayer before beginning the *Shema*.

בֵּין בְּגִלְגּוּל זֶה בֵּין בְּגִלְגּוּל אַחֵר — *Whether in*

this life or another life [lit., *this transmigration or another transmigration*].

This term *gilgul* refers to the doctrine of גִּלְגּוּל נְשָׁמוֹת, *transmigration of souls*, one of the most mystical doctrines in Kabbalistic literature. In very simple terms it refers to the reincarnation of certain souls for a second period of physical life on earth — in the case of the wicked to correct certain evil deeds, or in the case of the righteous to allow 'sparks' of his soul to enlighten subsequent generations. This concept also finds expression in the doctrine of *yibum* — levirate marriage, in which a childless widow marries a brother

⤐ The Bedtime Shema

Master of the Universe, I hereby forgive anyone who angered or an-
tagonized me or who sinned against me, whether against my body, my
property, my honor or against anything of mine; whether [he did so]
accidentally, willfully, carelessly, or purposely; whether through speech,
deed, thought, or notion; whether in this life or another life° — [I forgive]
every Jew. May no man be punished because of me. May it be Your will,
HASHEM, my God and the God of my forefathers, that I may sin no more
(nor repeat them, and may I not revert to angering You, and may I not do
what is evil in Your eyes). Whatever sins I have done before You, may You
blot out in Your abundant mercy, but not through suffering or bad illnesses.
Psalms May the expressions of my mouth and the thoughts of my heart find favor
19:15 before You, HASHEM, my Rock and my Redeemer.

Blessed are You, HASHEM, our God, King of the universe, Who casts
the bonds of sleep upon my eyes and slumber upon my eyelids°
(and Who illuminates the apple of the eye). May it be Your will,
HASHEM, my God and the God of my forefathers, that You lay me
down to sleep in peace° and raise me erect (for good life and) in peace.

---

of her deceased husband. As a result of
such a union, the soul of the dead brother
would become reincarnated in the child
born of the levirate union. See *Ramban* to
Genesis 38:8. [See also *Or Some'ach, Hil.
Teshuvah* 5 s.v. וְיָדַעְתִּי.]

הַמַּפִּיל / HaMapil

This benediction is of ancient origin. Its
text is a version of the one recorded in
Berachos 60b. The words in parentheses
are added in most *Nusach Sfard* siddurim.

There is a difference of opinion
regarding the sequence of the prayers. The
printed versions in most prayerbooks —
which we follow in this volume — has the
'HaMapil' benediction first and then the
Shema. This follows the order recorded by
Rambam Hilchos Tefillah 7:1. According
to *Shulchan Aruch* (*Orach Chaim* 239:1)
(apparently following the Talmud,
Berachos 60b) it is better to begin by
reciting the *Shema* and conclude with the
HaMapil benedictiòn. Since *HaMapil*
refers directly to the onset of slumber it
should be recited as close as possible to the
moment of sleep.

Some say *HaMapil* after *Shema* and then
recite the additional psalms and verses,
while others recite *HaMapil* at the very
end. The latter seems to be the more
prevalent custom (*Mishneh Berurah*
239:1:23; *Aruch HaShulchan*).

It is not proper to eat, drink, or talk after
reciting the *HaMapil* benediction; one

should go to sleep immediately thereafter.
In case one is unable to fall asleep
immediately one should repeat the passages
of the *Shema* and Psalms until sleep
overtakes him (*Derech HaChaim; Aruch
HaShulchan*).

הַמַּפִּיל חֶבְלֵי שֵׁנָה עַל עֵינַי וּתְנוּמָה עַל עַפְעַפָּי —
*Who casts the bonds of sleep upon my eyes
and slumber upon my eyelids.* This directly
corresponds to the benediction recited in
the morning: הַמַּעֲבִיר חֶבְלֵי שֵׁנָה מֵעֵינַי וּתְנוּמָה
מֵעַפְעַפָּי, *Who removes the bonds of sleep
from my eyes, and slumber from my
eyelids.* There we thank God for returning
us to active living; here we thank Him for
the gift of sleep (*World of Prayer*).

The expression *bonds of sleep*
figuratively depicts the whole body as
being securely chained in sleep. Others
render חֶבְלֵי שֵׁנָה as 'portion' of sleep [see
Deut. 32:9; *Chizkuni; Abudraham*].

This benediction and the corresponding
one of the morning are expressed in first-
person singular, because they are concerned with *personal* well-being [comp.,
however, *Magen Avraham* 46:4] (*R'
Hirsch*).

וּמֵאִיר לְאִישׁוֹן בַּת־עָיִן — *And Who
illuminates the apple of the eye.* See comm.
below s.v. הַמֵּאִיר, *Who illuminates.*)

שֶׁתַּשְׁכִּיבֵנִי לְשָׁלוֹם ... וְאַל יְבַהֲלוּנִי רַעְיוֹנַי —
*That You lay me down to sleep in peace ...
may my ideas ... not confound me.*

The benediction refers first to protection

חֶלְקִי בְּתוֹרָתֶךָ, וְתַרְגִּילֵנִי לִדְבַר מִצְוָה, וְאַל תַּרְגִּילֵנִי לִדְבַר
עֲבֵרָה: וְאַל תְּבִיאֵנִי לִידֵי חֵטְא, וְלֹא לִידֵי נִסָּיוֹן, וְלֹא לִידֵי
בִזָּיוֹן. וְיִשְׁלוֹט בִּי יֵצֶר הַטּוֹב, וְאַל יִשְׁלוֹט בִּי יֵצֶר הָרָע.
וְתַצִּילֵנִי מִשָּׂטָן וּמִפֶּגַע רָע, וּמֵחֳלָיִים רָעִים.) וְאַל יְבַהֲלוּנִי
רַעְיוֹנַי, וַחֲלוֹמוֹת רָעִים, וְהִרְהוּרִים רָעִים. וּתְהִי מִטָּתִי שְׁלֵמָה
לְפָנֶיךָ. וְהָאֵר עֵינַי פֶּן אִישַׁן הַמָּוֶת. כִּי־אַתָּה הַמֵּאִיר לְאִישׁוֹן
בַּת עָיִן. בָּרוּךְ אַתָּה יהוה, הַמֵּאִיר לָעוֹלָם כֻּלּוֹ בִּכְבוֹדוֹ.

אֵל מֶלֶךְ נֶאֱמָן:

שְׁמַע יִשְׂרָאֵל יהוה אֱלֹהֵינוּ יהוה | אֶחָד:

בָּרוּךְ שֵׁם כְּבוֹד מַלְכוּתוֹ לְעוֹלָם וָעֶד.

וְאָהַבְתָּ אֵת יהוה אֱלֹהֶיךָ בְּכָל־לְבָבְךָ וּבְכָל־נַפְשְׁךָ
וּבְכָל־מְאֹדֶךָ: וְהָיוּ הַדְּבָרִים הָאֵלֶּה אֲשֶׁר אָנֹכִי מְצַוְּךָ
הַיּוֹם עַל־לְבָבֶךָ: וְשִׁנַּנְתָּם לְבָנֶיךָ וְדִבַּרְתָּ בָּם בְּשִׁבְתְּךָ
בְּבֵיתֶךָ וּבְלֶכְתְּךָ בַדֶּרֶךְ וּבְשָׁכְבְּךָ וּבְקוּמֶךָ: וּקְשַׁרְתָּם
לְאוֹת עַל־יָדֶךָ וְהָיוּ לְטֹטָפֹת בֵּין עֵינֶיךָ: וּכְתַבְתָּם עַל־
מְזֻזוֹת בֵּיתֶךָ וּבִשְׁעָרֶיךָ:

וִיהִי נֹעַם אֲדֹנָי אֱלֹהֵינוּ עָלֵינוּ, וּמַעֲשֵׂה יָדֵינוּ כּוֹנְנָה עָלֵינוּ,
וּמַעֲשֵׂה יָדֵינוּ כּוֹנְנֵהוּ.

— שֶׁתַּשְׁכִּיבֵנִי לְשָׁלוֹם —
and next to thoughts menacing our peace
of mind and soul — וְאַל יְבַהֲלוּנִי גו׳. We pray
that the ideas and fantasies [רַעְיוֹנוֹת] that
we nurse in our wakeful hours not produce
disturbing nightmares or immoral dreams.
Such dreams menace the purity of our
thoughts and feelings even during our
waking (World of Prayer).

וּתְהִי מִטָּתִי שְׁלֵמָה — May my offspring be
perfect [lit. may my (conjugal) bed be
perfect]. The expression is of Talmudic
origin [Pesachim 56] and implies: Let all
my children be perfect. This expression
originally applied to the Patriarch Jacob
whose progeny were all righteous, unlike
Abraham and Isaac, each of whom
produced a wicked son — Ishmael and Esau
respectively. See Rashi to Genesis 47:31.

וְהָאֵר עֵינַי פֶּן אִישַׁן הַמָּוֶת — And may You
illuminate my eyes lest I die in sleep. See
Psalm 13:4, and the dictum in the Talmud
57b that "sleep is one-sixtieth of death."

The idea is that when asleep we are in a
state related to death and utter darkness,
but God guards our souls, as it were. We
now beseech Him to return us to a state of
vigorous and sparkling light on the
morrow lest we sleep the sleep of death.

הַמֵּאִיר לְאִישׁוֹן בַּת עָיִן — Who illuminates the
apple of the eye. The terms אִישׁוֹן and בַּת עָיִן
are essentially synonymous denoting the
pupil of the eye; idiomatically called the
"apple' of the eye. The expression is
borrowed from Psalms 17:8, שָׁמְרֵנִי כְּאִישׁוֹן
בַּת־עָיִן, guard me as the apple of Your eye.
[See ArtScroll comm.]

The idea is that when one craves sleep
the pupils of his eyes are figuratively
darkened; when one has slept and is fully
rested, his eyes are 'brightened'
(Abudraham).

⤶§ The Shema

[For all full phrase-by-phrase commentary see pages 14-31.]

The halachic practice is that one who

(Grant my share in Your Torah and accustom me toward good deeds but do not accustom me toward bad deeds. Do not deliver me to sin nor to challenge nor to humiliation. Cause the good inclination to dominate me but do not let the evil inclination dominate me. Rescue me from impediment, from evil attack, and from bad illnesses.) May my ideas, bad dreams, and bad notions not confound me;° may my offspring be perfect° before You, and may You illuminate my eyes lest I die in sleep [for it is You who illuminates the apple of the eye]. Blessed are You HASHEM, Who illuminates the entire world with His glory.

God, Trustworthy King

Deuteronomy 6:4
Hear, O Israel: HASHEM is [now] our God, HASHEM [will be] One.

Pesachim 56a   Blessed be the Name of His glorious kingdom for all eternity.

Deuteronomy 6:5-9
You shall love HASHEM, your God, with all your heart and with all your soul and with all your resources. Let these matters, which I command you today, be upon your heart. Teach them thoroughly to your children and speak of them while you sit in your home, while you walk on the way, when you recline and when you arise. Bind them as a sign upon your arm and they shall be tefillin between your eyes. And write them on the doorposts of your house and upon your gates.

Psalms 90:17
May the pleasantness of my Lord, our God, be upon us° — may He establish our handiwork for us;° our handiwork may He establish.

had recited the evening *Shema* in the *Maariv* service in its proper time [i.e. after the stars were out] now recites only the first portion of *Shema;* one who recited the *Maariv* service before nightfall [i.e., before it is quite dark] should recite all three portions of *Shema.* According to some authorities, all three portions of *Shema* should be repeated every night before retiring whether or not *Maariv* was recited in its ideal time since the 248 words of the entire *Shema* have a beneficial effect in protecting one's organs [see comm. on page 14]. However, since the Talmud (*Berachos* 60b) mentions only the first section, that suffices [except in the case of early *Maariv* as noted above, when all three portions must be recited] (*Aruch HaShulchan, Orach Chaim 239; see Abudraham; Rashi Berachos 2a*).

◆§ יֵשֵׁב בְּסֵתֶר ... וִיהִי נֹעַם / **Psalms 90:17 —** 91.

The recital of this psalm, as well as *Psalm 3,* before retiring is mentioned in the Talmud (*Shevuos* 15b). This psalm is described by the Talmud (*Shavuos* 15b) as שִׁיר שֶׁל פְּגָעִים, *Song Against Evil Occurrences,* or שִׁיר שֶׁל נְגָעִים, *Song Against Plagues.* It is a plea for protection from all harmful forces and influences. [See also *Rambam, Hil. Avodas Cochavim* 11:12.]

The verse וִיהִי נֹעַם, *May the pleasantness,* is the closing sentence of Psalm 90 which begins תְּפִלָּה לְמֹשֶׁה, *A prayer of Moses.* It was composed by Moses when the Tabernacle was completed. In the final verse he offered a short plea that our service of God be pleasing to Him and its effects be permanent, a fitting

יֵשֵׁב בְּסֵתֶר עֶלְיוֹן, בְּצֵל שַׁדַּי יִתְלוֹנָן. אֹמַר לַיהוה, מַחְסִי
וּמְצוּדָתִי, אֱלֹהַי אֶבְטַח־בּוֹ. כִּי הוּא יַצִּילְךָ מִפַּח יָקוּשׁ,
מִדֶּבֶר הַוּוֹת. בְּאֶבְרָתוֹ יָסֶךְ לָךְ, וְתַחַת־כְּנָפָיו תֶּחְסֶה, צִנָּה
וְסֹחֵרָה אֲמִתּוֹ. לֹא־תִירָא מִפַּחַד לָיְלָה, מֵחֵץ יָעוּף יוֹמָם.
מִדֶּבֶר בָּאֹפֶל יַהֲלֹךְ, מִקֶּטֶב יָשׁוּד צָהֳרָיִם. יִפֹּל מִצִּדְּךָ אֶלֶף,
וּרְבָבָה מִימִינֶךָ, אֵלֶיךָ לֹא יִגָּשׁ. רַק בְּעֵינֶיךָ תַבִּיט, וְשִׁלֻּמַת
רְשָׁעִים תִּרְאֶה. כִּי־אַתָּה יהוה מַחְסִי, עֶלְיוֹן שַׂמְתָּ מְעוֹנֶךָ. לֹא
תְאֻנֶּה אֵלֶיךָ רָעָה, וְנֶגַע לֹא־יִקְרַב בְּאָהֳלֶךָ. כִּי מַלְאָכָיו יְצַוֶּה־
לָךְ, לִשְׁמָרְךָ בְּכָל־דְּרָכֶיךָ. עַל־כַּפַּיִם יִשָּׂאוּנְךָ, פֶּן־תִּגֹּף בָּאֶבֶן
רַגְלֶךָ. עַל־שַׁחַל וָפֶתֶן תִּדְרֹךְ, תִּרְמֹס כְּפִיר וְתַנִּין. כִּי בִי חָשַׁק
וַאֲפַלְּטֵהוּ, אֲשַׂגְּבֵהוּ, כִּי־יָדַע שְׁמִי. יִקְרָאֵנִי וְאֶעֱנֵהוּ, עִמּוֹ־אָנֹכִי
בְצָרָה, אֲחַלְּצֵהוּ וַאֲכַבְּדֵהוּ. אֹרֶךְ יָמִים אַשְׂבִּיעֵהוּ, וְאַרְאֵהוּ
בִּישׁוּעָתִי. אֹרֶךְ יָמִים אַשְׂבִּיעֵהוּ, וְאַרְאֵהוּ בִּישׁוּעָתִי.

יהוה מָה־רַבּוּ צָרָי, רַבִּים קָמִים עָלָי. רַבִּים אֹמְרִים לְנַפְשִׁי,
אֵין יְשׁוּעָתָה לּוֹ בֵאלֹהִים סֶלָה. וְאַתָּה יהוה מָגֵן

prayer for recital before retiring.

Psalm 91, another one of the Psalms attributed to Moses, forms a comprehensive prayer for safeguarding us from all perils. Accordingly, it is an appropriate prayer before retiring, especially because of v. 5: *You shall not fear the terror of night.*

[The comments to the *Psalms* that follow have been gleaned primarily from the ArtScroll *Tehillim*, by Rabbi Avrohom Chaim Feuer. Refer to that work for a full commentary to the various psalms.]

וִיהִי נֹעַם ה' אֱלֹהֵינוּ — *May the pleasantness of my Lord, our God.* The term נֹעַם, *pleasantness*, refers to the bliss someone feels when he has done something that achieved its purpose. When man has this feeling of accomplishment, he is not alone — God, too, feels satisfaction that His will has been done (*Malbim*).

וּמַעֲשֵׂה יָדֵינוּ כּוֹנְנָה עָלֵינוּ — *May He establish our handiwork for us.* In any material activity, a craftsman shapes his creation, but remains dependent on it, in a sense. Architects and builders can erect a structure, but it rests on the earth, not on them, and *they* must depend on *it* for shelter. In the spiritual world, the opposite is true. One's Torah study develops in his own mind and his performance of a *mitzvah* has as much spiritual content as he

puts into it. We pray now that our deeds be worthy of God's pleasure and that he 'establish' them as being significant (*Malbim*).

יֵשֵׁב בְּסֵתֶר ◆§ / Psalm 91

יֵשֵׁב בְּסֵתֶר עֶלְיוֹן — *Whoever sits in the refuge* [lit. *hidden or secret place*] *of the Most High.* The person who scorns conventional forms of protection and seeks only the refuge provided by the Most High will find his faith rewarded. He will be enveloped by God's providence so that he can continue to seek holiness and wisdom without fear of those who would seek to harm him: *He shall dwell in the shadow of the Almighty* (*Rashi*).

אֹמַר לַה' מַחְסִי וּמְצוּדָתִי — *I will say of HASHEM; He is my refuge and my fortress.* The devout man who *dwells in the secret place of the Most High* declares publicly that God is his *refuge* from all physical dangers, and his *fortress*, protecting him from all human enemies (*Radak; Sforno*).

לֹא תִירָא מִפַּחַד לָיְלָה — *You shall not fear the terror of night.* If you put your faith in God, fear will be banished from your heart (*Rashi*).

וְנֶגַע לֹא יִקְרַב בְּאָהֳלֶךָ — *Nor will any plague come near your tent.* The Talmud (*Sanhedrin* 103a) perceives this as a

Psalm 91 Whoever sits in the refuge of the Most High° — he shall dwell in the shadow of the Almighty. I will say of HASHEM; He is my refuge and my fortress,° my God — I will trust in Him. That He will deliver you from the ensnaring trap and from devastating pestilence. With His pinion He will cover you, and beneath His wings you will be protected; His truth will be a shield and armor. You shall not fear the terror of night,° nor the arrow that flies by day; nor the pestilence that walks in gloom, nor the destroyer who lays waste at noon. A thousand will fall at your side and a myriad at your right hand, but to you it shall not approach. You will merely peer with your eyes and you will see the retribution of the wicked. Because 'You, HASHEM, are my refuge,' You have made the Most High Your dwelling place. No evil will befall you, nor will any plague come near your tent.° He will charge His angels for you, to protect you in all your ways.° They will carry you on their palms,° lest you strike your foot against a stone. You will tread upon the lion and the viper, you will trample the young lion and the serpent. For he has yearned for Me and I will deliver him; I will elevate him because he knows My Name. He will call upon Me and I will answer him, I am with him in distress, I will release him and I will honor him I will satisfy him with long life and show him My salvation. I will satisfy him with long life and show him My salvation.°

Psalms 3:2-9 HASHEM, how many are my tormentors!° The great rise up against me! The great say of my soul, 'There is no salvation for him from God.' Selah!° But you HASHEM are a shield for me — for my soul, and

blessing for domestic bliss [for *tent* signifies 'household']. 'May you raise worthy children and students who will not shame you by acting improperly in public.'

לִשְׁמָרְךָ בְּכָל דְּרָכֶיךָ — *To protect you in all your ways.* The Talmud (Chagigah 16a) teaches that these angels are not merely guardians, but witnesses as well. They observe every action and they are destined to testify for or against the man under their protection when he comes before the heavenly tribunal after death.

עַל כַּפַּיִם יִשָּׂאוּנְךָ — *They will carry you on* [their] *palms.* The angels created by the *mitzvos* that you perform with your *palms* [i.e., giving charity and doing acts of kindness] will raise you above all dangers that lurk in your path (*Zera Yaakov*).

וְאַרְאֵהוּ בִּישׁוּעָתִי — *And* [I will] *show him My salvation.* He will live to personally witness the salvation I will bring about at the advent of the Messiah, at the time of the revival of the dead, and at the salvation of the World to Come (*Radak*).
Indeed, it is not God who needs

salvation, but Israel; yet God calls Israel's victory 'My salvation' to emphasize that Israel's salvation is His as well (*Midrash Shocher Tov*). It is God's desire to display His Presence in this world, but if there were no Israel, no community of faith, then there would be no place for God to reveal His glory and no one to appreciate Him. Therefore, God, Himself, is the beneficiary of Israel's salvation (*Tehillos Hashem*).
There are Kabbalistic reasons for repeating the last verse. See *Likutei Mahariach.*

◆§ ה' מָה רַבּוּ צָרָי / **Psalm 3**
This psalm was composed by David, as its first verse states, " ... *When he* [*David*] *fled from Absalom his son*," as he perceived through Divine inspiration that his salvation was forthcoming. Verse 6 — *I lay down and slept; yet I awoke, for HASHEM supports me —* makes this psalm especially appropriate for the night.
A full appreciation of this psalm is impossible without knowing the historical background of Absalom's revolt. See *II Samuel* chapters 15-19 for the full details.

בַּעֲדִי, כְּבוֹדִי וּמֵרִים רֹאשִׁי. קוֹלִי אֶל־יהוה אֶקְרָא, וַיַּעֲנֵנִי מֵהַר
קָדְשׁוֹ סֶלָה. אֲנִי שָׁכַבְתִּי וָאִישָׁנָה, הֱקִיצוֹתִי, כִּי יהוה יִסְמְכֵנִי.
לֹא־אִירָא מֵרִבְבוֹת עָם, אֲשֶׁר סָבִיב שָׁתוּ עָלָי. קוּמָה יהוה,
הוֹשִׁיעֵנִי אֱלֹהַי, כִּי הִכִּיתָ אֶת־כָּל־אֹיְבַי לֶחִי, שִׁנֵּי רְשָׁעִים
שִׁבַּרְתָּ. לַיהוה הַיְשׁוּעָה, עַל־עַמְּךָ בִרְכָתֶךָ סֶּלָה.

הַשְׁכִּיבֵנוּ יהוה אֱלֹהֵינוּ לְשָׁלוֹם, וְהַעֲמִידֵנוּ מַלְכֵּנוּ לְחַיִּים
(טוֹבִים וּלְשָׁלוֹם). וּפְרוֹשׂ עָלֵינוּ סֻכַּת שְׁלוֹמֶךָ.
וְתַקְּנֵנוּ בְּעֵצָה טוֹבָה מִלְּפָנֶיךָ. וְהוֹשִׁיעֵנוּ (מְהֵרָה) לְמַעַן שְׁמֶךָ.
וְהָגֵן בַּעֲדֵנוּ, וְהָסֵר מֵעָלֵינוּ אוֹיֵב דֶּבֶר וְחֶרֶב וְרָעָב וְיָגוֹן. וְהָסֵר
שָׂטָן מִלְּפָנֵינוּ וּמֵאַחֲרֵינוּ. וּבְצֵל כְּנָפֶיךָ תַּסְתִּירֵנוּ. כִּי אֵל
שׁוֹמְרֵנוּ וּמַצִּילֵנוּ אָתָּה, כִּי אֵל מֶלֶךְ חַנּוּן וְרַחוּם אָתָּה. וּשְׁמוֹר
צֵאתֵנוּ וּבוֹאֵנוּ לְחַיִּים וּלְשָׁלוֹם, מֵעַתָּה וְעַד עוֹלָם.

בָּרוּךְ יהוה בַּיּוֹם, בָּרוּךְ יהוה בַּלַּיְלָה, בָּרוּךְ יהוה בְּשָׁכְבֵנוּ,
בָּרוּךְ יהוה בְּקוּמֵנוּ. כִּי בְיָדְךָ נַפְשׁוֹת הַחַיִּים וְהַמֵּתִים.
אֲשֶׁר בְּיָדוֹ נֶפֶשׁ כָּל־חָי, וְרוּחַ כָּל־בְּשַׂר־אִישׁ. בְּיָדְךָ אַפְקִיד
רוּחִי, פָּדִיתָה אוֹתִי, יהוה אֵל אֱמֶת. אֱלֹהֵינוּ שֶׁבַּשָּׁמַיִם, יַחֵד
שִׁמְךָ וְקַיֵּם מַלְכוּתְךָ תָּמִיד, וּמְלוֹךְ עָלֵינוּ לְעוֹלָם וָעֶד.

סֶלָה — Selah. This word is one of the most difficult in Scripture. *Targum* and *Metzudas Zion* render it *'forever'*, thus we read here 'there is no salvation ... forever,' a view that is supported by the Talmud (Eruvin 54a).

Ibn Ezra maintains that the word סֶלָה is always a reaffirmation of a preceding statement, i.e. 'all of the aforementioned is *true and certain.' Ibn Ezra* and *Radak* offer an alternate meaning that *'selah'* is a musical instruction addressed to the singers of the psalm. It indicates special emphasis and a raising of the voice.

קוֹלִי אֶל ה׳ אֶקְרָא וַיַּעֲנֵנִי — *With my voice I call out to HASHEM, and he answers* [lit. 'would or did answer'] *me.*

Ibn Ezra connects this verse to the preceding one. David sees God as his shield because he knows that to win he need not even enter into battle; rather, he assures his victory by calling out sincerely to God.

וַיַּעֲנֵנִי — *And he answers me* [lit. 'He did answer me']. The word literally is in past tense. David had so much confidence in God's response that whenever he prayed he

was sure that his wish would be fulfilled. It was as if God had *already* answered his request (*Radak*).

אֲנִי שָׁכַבְתִּי וָאִישָׁנָה — *I lay down and* [I] *slept.* In the darkest hour of his despair, David was numb with fear, so he retreated into senseless sleep (*Rashi*).

הֱקִיצוֹתִי — *Yet I awoke!* From my worries I awoke triumphantly, filled with confidence that God would support me (*Rashi*).

קוּמָה ה׳ הוֹשִׁיעֵנִי אֱלֹהַי — *Rise up, HASHEM, save me, my God!* Because I have unshakeable faith in You, it is only proper that You save me (*Metzudos*).

עַל עַמְּךָ בִרְכָתֶךָ — *Upon Your people is* [i.e. their duty is] *Your blessing.* I.e., to bless You and to offer thanks for Your salvation (*Rashi*). [God derives strength, so to speak, from the blessings and prayers of man. Man's appreciation of God's control of human events influences His guidance of the universe.]

◆§ הַשְׁכִּיבֵנוּ / **Hashkiveinu**

This prayer from the *Maariv* service describes God as our Savior from the

to raise up my pride. With my voice I call out to HASHEM, and He answers me° from His holy mountain. Selah. I lay down and slept;° yet I awoke,° for HASHEM supports me. I fear not the myriad people deployed against me from every side. Rise up, HASHEM, save me, My God!° For You struck all of my enemies on the cheek, You broke the teeth of the wicked. Salvation is HASHEM's, upon Your people is Your blessing.° Selah.

Siddur
Maariv

Lay us down to sleep in peace,° HASHEM, our God; raise us erect, our King, to (good) life (and peace), and spread over us° the shelter of Your peace. Set us aright with good counsel from before Your presence, and save us (speedily) for Your Name's sake. Shield us, remove from us foe, plague, sword, famine, and woe; and remove spiritual impediment from before us and behind us° and shelter us in the shadow of Your wings — for God Who protects us and rescues us are You, for God Who is the merciful and compassionate King are You. Safeguard our going and coming — for life and peace, from now to eternity.

Siddur
Maariv

Job 12:10

Psalms 31:6

Blessed is HASHEM by day,° blessed is HASHEM by night. Blessed is HASHEM when we retire, blessed is HASHEM when we arise — for in Your hand are the souls of the living and the dead: The One in whose hand is the soul of all the living and the spirit of all human flesh. In Your hand I entrust my spirit,° You redeemed me HASHEM, O God of truth. Our God Who is in heaven, reveal the Oneness of Your Name, establish Your kingdom forever, and reign over us for all eternity.

dangers and afflictions associated with the terrors of night, literally and figuratively (*Seder HaYom*).

הַשְׁכִּיבֵנוּ ... לְשָׁלוֹם — *Lay us down to sleep in peace.* The purpose of sleep is to allow the body to rejuvenate itself, the better to serve God the next day (*R' Hirsch*).

וּפְרוֹשׁ עָלֵינוּ — *And spread over us.* At night the commandment of *tzitzis* does not apply, so we are denuded of the *mitzvah* that envelops us in the daytime. In its absence, we ask God to 'spread a protective blessing of peace over us' (*Midrash Tehillim* 86:1).

וְתַקְּנֵנוּ בְּעֵצָה טוֹבָה — *Set us aright with good counsel.* Help us plan well at night for the activity of the next day, and let the relaxation of the night give us a clearer perspective for the deliberations of the day (*R' Hirsch*).

מִלְּפָנֵינוּ וּמֵאַחֲרֵינוּ — *From before us and behind us.* Protect us from spiritual harm in the future [*before us*] and from the consequences of what has already occurred [*behind us*] (*R' Hirsch*).

When we plan for the future, the Evil Inclination has endless arguments to convince us that sin is advantageous and virtue is archaic. When we seek to repent our misdeeds of the past, he argues that 'everyone' did the same thing and it is too late to cry over spilt milk (*Siach Yitzchak*).

◆§ בָּרוּךְ ה' בַּיּוֹם / **Additional verses**
These passages which concentrate on human praise and supplication are essentially repeated from the *Maariv* service. The Talmud [*Berachos* 4a; see *Tosafos*] describes them as גְּאוּלָה אֲרִיכְתָּא, extensions of the preceding blessing of redemption. The full prayer beginning בָּרוּךְ ה' לְעוֹלָם contains eighteen Divine Names, to parallel the eighteen benedictions in *Shemoneh Esrei*. The verses proclaim the incomparable glory, love, and justice of God, and pray for the recognition of Divine Unity by all peoples.

בְּיָדְךָ אַפְקִיד רוּחִי ... — *In Your hand I entrust my spirit ...* [*Psalms* 31:6]. The Talmud (*Berachos* 5a) puts this verse in the category of פְּסוּקֵי דְרַחֲמֵי, *verses of Divine Mercy*.

יִרְאוּ עֵינֵינוּ, וְיִשְׂמַח לִבֵּנוּ, וְתָגֵל נַפְשֵׁנוּ בִּישׁוּעָתְךָ בֶּאֱמֶת, בֶּאֱמֹר לְצִיּוֹן מָלַךְ אֱלֹהָיִךְ. יהוה מֶלֶךְ, יהוה מָלָךְ, יהוה יִמְלֹךְ לְעֹלָם וָעֶד. כִּי הַמַּלְכוּת שֶׁלְּךָ הִיא, וּלְעוֹלְמֵי עַד תִּמְלוֹךְ בְּכָבוֹד, כִּי אֵין לָנוּ מֶלֶךְ אֶלָּא אָתָּה.

הַמַּלְאָךְ הַגֹּאֵל אֹתִי מִכָּל־רָע יְבָרֵךְ אֶת־הַנְּעָרִים, וְיִקָּרֵא בָהֶם שְׁמִי וְשֵׁם אֲבֹתַי אַבְרָהָם וְיִצְחָק, וְיִדְגּוּ לָרֹב בְּקֶרֶב הָאָרֶץ.

וַיֹּאמֶר, אִם־שָׁמוֹעַ תִּשְׁמַע לְקוֹל יהוה אֱלֹהֶיךָ, וְהַיָּשָׁר בְּעֵינָיו תַּעֲשֶׂה, וְהַאֲזַנְתָּ לְמִצְוֹתָיו, וְשָׁמַרְתָּ כָּל־חֻקָּיו, כָּל־הַמַּחֲלָה אֲשֶׁר־שַׂמְתִּי בְמִצְרַיִם לֹא־אָשִׂים עָלֶיךָ, כִּי אֲנִי יהוה רֹפְאֶךָ.

וַיֹּאמֶר יהוה אֶל־הַשָּׂטָן, יִגְעַר יהוה בְּךָ הַשָּׂטָן, וְיִגְעַר יהוה בְּךָ הַבֹּחֵר בִּירוּשָׁלָיִם, הֲלוֹא זֶה אוּד מֻצָּל מֵאֵשׁ.

הִנֵּה מִטָּתוֹ שֶׁלִּשְׁלֹמֹה, שִׁשִּׁים גִּבֹּרִים סָבִיב לָהּ, מִגִּבֹּרֵי יִשְׂרָאֵל. כֻּלָּם אֲחֻזֵי חֶרֶב, מְלֻמְּדֵי מִלְחָמָה, אִישׁ חַרְבּוֹ

The *Zohar* comments: Every night when we go to sleep we entrust ourselves to God. Although our debt to God is great, He does not hold back the soul as payment. He is אֱמֶת, *true*, to His role as Guardian of souls, and returns them in the morning (*Ketzos HaChoshen* 4:1).

◈§ יִרְאוּ עֵינֵינוּ / *Yir'u Eineinu*

This collection of prayers is also borrowed from the *Maariv* service. It expresses the hope of the speedy establishment of HASHEM's kingdom.

◈§ הַמַּלְאָךְ / **The angel**

The following passages are a collection of Scriptural verses discussing God's "mercy." This first verse, *May the angel who redeems*, etc. was Jacob's blessing to his grandsons Ephraim and Manasseh [*Genesis* 48:16].

The prayer is directed not to the angel, who has no power except as an agent of God, but to God Who dispatched the angel. The sense is: *May it be pleasing to You that the angel whom you have always dispatched to redeem me from all evil shall bless the lads.* [For a full exposition of this verse, see ArtScroll *Genesis* 48:16.]

וְיִקָּרֵא בָהֶם שְׁמִי וכו' — *And may my name be declared upon them, and the names of my forefathers Abraham and Isaac.* May they

constantly strive to such heights that they will be worthy to have their names coupled with those of the Patriarchs (*R' Avraham b. HaRambam*).

Haamek Davar comments that the invocation of the three Patriarchs was intended to invoke God's blessing in three areas: military security, livelihood, and internal peace and harmony.

וְיִדְגּוּ לָרֹב בְּקֶרֶב הָאָרֶץ — *And may they proliferate abundantly like fish within the land.*

Like fish — which are fruitful and which multiply, and which the Evil Eye cannot affect [since fish live in an element apart, in calm and unseen depths. Mankind, inhabitants of another element, remain unaware of this aquatic existence, and so do not cast an evil eye upon them. And in any event, the Evil Eye has no effect over what is hidden from sight (see *Berachos* 20a)]. So will Joseph's descendants multiply and be unharmed by the Evil Eye (*Rashi*). As *R' Hirsch* explains in his *Siddur* (p. 726), just as fish enjoy a quiet but contented and cheerful life beyond the conception of human beings, so Jews who live in the sphere assigned them by God will have a degree of serenity and happiness far beyond the comprehension

Siddur Maariv **M**ay our eyes see,° our heart be glad, and our soul exult in Your true salvation — when Zion is told, 'your God has reigned!' HASHEM reigns, HASHEM has reigned, HASHEM will reign for all eternity. For the kingdom is Yours and You will reign for all eternity in glory for we have no king except for You!

Genesis 48:16 **M**ay the angel° who redeems me from all evil bless the lads, and may my name be declared upon them, and the names of my forefathers Abraham and Isaac,° and may they proliferate abundantly like fish° within the land.

Exodus 15:26 **H**e said, 'If you diligently heed° the voice of HASHEM, your God, and do what is proper in His eyes, and you listen closely to His commandments and observe His decrees° — the entire malady that I inflicted upon Egypt° I will not inflict upon you, for I am HASHEM your Healer.'°

Zechariah 3:2 **H**ASHEM said to the Satan,° 'HASHEM shall denounce you, O Satan, and HASHEM, Who selects Jerusalem, shall denounce you again. This is indeed a firebrand rescued from flames.'

Song of Songs 3:7-8 **B**ehold! The couch of Shlomo! Sixty mighty ones round about it, of the mighty ones of Israel. All gripping the sword, learned in

of those around them.

וַיֹּאמֶר אִם שָׁמוֹעַ תִּשְׁמַע §◄ / He said, 'If you diligently heed.'

This passage, from *Exodus 15:26*, was the Divine exhortation that Moses imparted to the Jewish nation when it began its arduous journey through the wilderness after being freed from Egyptian slavery. This verse forms the basis for the Talmudic statement [*Berachos* 5a] that Torah-study, no less than the reading of the *Shema*, wards off danger (*World of Prayer*).

חֻקָּיו — *His decrees.* These are the commandments which take the form of royal decrees with no reason assigned for their performance (*Rashi*).

כָּל הַמַּחֲלָה אֲשֶׁר שַׂמְתִּי בְמִצְרַיִם — *The entire malady that I inflicted upon Egypt.* I.e., the plagues. If the Jews remain loyal, they will be spared physical affliction (*Ramban*).

אֲנִי ה' רֹפְאֶךָ — *I am HASHEM your Healer.* From ills from which no physician can cure you (*Ibn Ezra*). [That is, God is the Primary Healer.]

— I instruct you that My Commandments will protect you from disease, like a physician who warns against eating something which would cause an illness (*Rashi*).

The clause is contingent: *If you will*

diligently heed, I will not bring diseases upon you; but if you do not *heed*, I will. Nevertheless — *I am HASHEM Who heals you* [the diseases will not be incurable, as were those that God brought upon Egypt (*Torah Temimah*)] (*Talmud Sanhedrin* 101a).

וַיֹּאמֶר ה' אֶל הַשָּׂטָן §◄ / And HASHEM said to the Satan

This passage occurs in *Zechariah 3:2* where the Prophet is shown a vision of *Joshua the High Priest standing before an angel of God, and the Satan* [accusing angel] *was standing at his right to accuse him.* The Satan accused Joshua of being too permissive with his sinful children, and of hindering the rebuilding of the Temple. Thereupon God — "Who chose Jerusalem" — rebuked Satan, reminding him that Joshua was like a *firebrand plucked out of the fire.* That is, Joshua had been Divinely vindicated inasmuch as he had been miraculously spared from the fires of Nebuchadnezzar. On a national level, the metaphor applies to the Jews as a whole. They, too, are like firebrands plucked from fire, for they had suffered from the fires of exile and endured it. They now merit redemption, not further accusation.

הִנֵּה מִטָּתוֹ §◄ / Behold! The couch

This passage from *Song of Songs* (3:7-8; see *Commentary* in the ArtScroll edition

עַל־יְרֵכוֹ מִפַּחַד בַּלֵּילוֹת.

יְבָרֶכְךָ יהוה וְיִשְׁמְרֶךָ. יָאֵר יהוה פָּנָיו אֵלֶיךָ, וִיחֻנֶּךָּ. יִשָּׂא יהוה פָּנָיו אֵלֶיךָ, וְיָשֵׂם לְךָ שָׁלוֹם.

הִנֵּה לֹא־יָנוּם וְלֹא יִישָׁן, שׁוֹמֵר יִשְׂרָאֵל.

לִישׁוּעָתְךָ קִוִּיתִי יהוה. קִוִּיתִי יהוה לִישׁוּעָתְךָ. יהוה לִישׁוּעָתְךָ קִוִּיתִי.

בְּשֵׁם יהוה אֱלֹהֵי יִשְׂרָאֵל, מִימִינִי מִיכָאֵל, וּמִשְּׂמֹאלִי גַּבְרִיאֵל, וּמִלְּפָנַי אוּרִיאֵל, וּמֵאֲחוֹרַי רְפָאֵל, וְעַל־רֹאשִׁי שְׁכִינַת אֵל.

שִׁיר הַמַּעֲלוֹת, אַשְׁרֵי כָּל־יְרֵא יהוה, הַהֹלֵךְ בִּדְרָכָיו. יְגִיעַ כַּפֶּיךָ כִּי תֹאכֵל, אַשְׁרֶיךָ וְטוֹב לָךְ. אֶשְׁתְּךָ

for the full literal and allegorical interpretation) refers allegorically to the Jewish people symbolized by the sixty myriads (i.e., the 600,000 mighty battleworthy males) who emerged from Egypt. They are fortified by their allegiance to the Torah, even in exile.

The Midrash comments on this passage: "When a man has yet to sin, his fellow beings on earth stand in awe of him, but once he has sinned he himself is overcome by fear and dread of others."

Its inclusion in the bedtime *Shema,* and its juxtaposition with the verses of the Priestly benediction (see below) is based on the Midrash (*Bamidbar Rabbah* 11:3).

Behold! The couch of Shlomo — Shlomo refers to God, because he is the Master of *Shalom* [peace] ...

Sixty mighty ones round about it — *God's couch* is figuratively surrounded by the sixty letters contained in *Bircas Kohanim;* **of the mighty ones of Israel** — for the blessings strengthen Israel.

All gripping the sword, learned in warfare — these blessings protect Israel against all retributions mentioned in the Torah.

Each with his sword on his thigh, from fear in the nights — if one dreams that a sword is cutting the flesh from his thigh, he should hurry to the synagogue and stand before the *Kohanim* to hear their blessing. Then no evil will befall him.

◆§ יְבָרֶכְךָ / Bircas Kohanim; the Priestly benediction [*Numbers* 6:24-26]

The blessing contains sixty letters; this has significant Kabbalistic meaning in its parallel with the sixty myriads of the previous passage. [For a full exposition of this blessing, see ArtScroll *Bircas Kohanim.* A sampling follows:]

May HASHEM bless you — with long life and wealth (Rashi; Ibn Ezra);

And safeguard you — guard you against robbery (ibid.);

May HASHEM illuminate His countenance for you — reveal to you the light of the Torah [i.e., endow you with spiritual growth] (Sifre); or, grant you children who will be Torah scholars (Tanchuma); may He answer your prayers and fulfill your requests (Ibn Ezra);

And be gracious to you — may He cause you to find grace [חֵן] in the eyes of others (Sifre); ... in the eyes of God (Ramban);

May HASHEM lift up His face toward you — i.e., may He always be favorably disposed towards you (Ibn Ezra).

And establish peace for you — peaceful relations with everyone (Midrash); spiritual eternity and perfection (Sforno). Peace is not simply the absence of war ... within man, it is the proper balance between the needs of the body and its higher duty to the soul (Or HaChaim).

Beloved is peace, since even the Priestly Benediction concludes with the hope of

warfare, each with his sword on his thigh, from fear in the nights.

Numbers
6:24-26 **M**ay HASHEM bless you and safeguard you.° May HASHEM illuminate His countenance for you and be gracious to you.° May HASHEM lift up His face toward you and establish peace for you.°

Psalms
121:4 **B**ehold, the Guardian of Israel neither slumbers nor sleeps.°

Genesis
49:18 **F**or Your salvation do I long, HASHEM.° I do long, HASHEM, for your salvation. HASHEM, for Your salvation do I long.

In the Name of HASHEM,° God of Israel: may Michael be at my right, Gabriel at my left, Uriel before me, and Raphael behind me; and above my head the Presence of God.

Psalm 128 **A** song of ascents.° Praiseworthy is everyone who fears HASHEM, who walks in his paths. When you eat the labor of your hands,° you are fortunate° and it is well with you. Your wife shall be like a

peace, thus teaching that blessings are of no avail unless accompanied by peace (*Midrash*).

[The three-fold repetition of these passages indicated in some *Siddurim* is Kabbalistic in origin. Occupation of a house for three years or a farm for three seasons constitutes proof of ownership (חֲזָקָה), and an animal's three-time commission of violent, aberrant behavior identifies it as a habitual menace. Similarly, the three-fold repetition of these verses symbolize the hope that these blessings will become permanently Israel's.]

§⊷ הִנֵּה לֹא יָנוּם / **Behold, the Guardian of Israel neither slumbers nor sleeps.**

— And therefore you will be able to sleep peacefully without fear of harm (*R' Hirsch*).

§⊷ לִישׁוּעָתְךָ קִוִּיתִי ה׳ / **For Your salvation do I long, HASHEM.**

This three-word prayer was originally uttered by the Patriarch Jacob in his blessing of his son Dan [*Genesis* 49:18]. As the commentators explain, it means: "I do not rely on temporary salvation through human agency; I await *Your* salvation — which will be for all eternity." [See ArtScroll *Bereishis* p. 2167.]

R' Bachya writes that the Kabbalists find in this three-word prayer mystical combinations of letters spelling the Divine Name that provides salvation against enemies. In order to arrive at the combination of letters yielding this Name, the three words of this prayer must be recited in different orders. The common custom is to recite it in the *Krias Shma* before going to sleep as follows: לִישׁוּעָתְךָ

קִוִּיתִי ה׳, קִוִּיתִי ה׳ לִישׁוּעָתְךָ, ה׳ לִישׁוּעָתְךָ קִוִּיתִי. However, some infer that *R' Bachya* prefers a different order (see *Chavel* ed.), and *Sh'lah* requires six variations of the verse: לִישׁוּעָתְךָ קִוִּיתִי ה׳, לִישׁוּעָתְךָ ה׳ קִוִּיתִי, קִוִּיתִי ה׳ לִישׁוּעָתְךָ, קִוִּיתִי לִישׁוּעָתְךָ ה׳, ה׳ לִישׁוּעָתְךָ קִוִּיתִי.

§⊷ בְּשֵׁם ה׳ / **In the Name of HASHEM**

God's angels surround you at His command: Michael, performing His unique miracles; Gabriel, the emissary of His almighty power; Uriel, who bears the light of God before you; Raphael, who brings you healing from Him. Above your head is the Presence of God Himself (*R' Hirsch*).

The Kabbalistic connotation of this arrangement, with man in the center, beneath God, is that the righteous act as God's 'chariot,' so to speak, bearing His glory on earth (*Iyun Tefillah*).

§⊷ שִׁיר הַמַּעֲלוֹת / **Psalm 128**

This Psalm is recited in the night-prayer, because, according to the Talmud (*Berachos* 57a), the two images depicted in it — the vine and olive shoots — are good omens for those to whom they appear in a dream [*Mateh Moshe* §401] (*World of Prayer*).

At night, we pause from the travail of the day and our hearts can open to yearnings and hopes for something better. This psalm depicts the joy of an ideal Jewish home, the sort of happiness toward which we should dedicate ourselves (*R' Hirsch*).

יְגִיעַ כַּפֶּיךָ כִּי תֹאכֵל — *When you eat the labor of your hands.* Honest labor benefits both

כְּגֶפֶן פֹּרִיָּה בְּיַרְכְּתֵי בֵיתֶךָ, בָּנֶיךָ כִּשְׁתִלֵי זֵיתִים, סָבִיב לְשֻׁלְחָנֶךָ. הִנֵּה כִי־כֵן יְבֹרַךְ גָּבֶר, יְרֵא יהוה. יְבָרֶכְךָ יהוה מִצִּיּוֹן, וּרְאֵה בְּטוּב יְרוּשָׁלָיִם כֹּל יְמֵי חַיֶּיךָ. וּרְאֵה־בָנִים לְבָנֶיךָ, שָׁלוֹם עַל־יִשְׂרָאֵל.

רִגְזוּ וְאַל־תֶּחֱטָאוּ, אִמְרוּ בִלְבַבְכֶם עַל מִשְׁכַּבְכֶם, וְדֹמּוּ סֶלָה.

אֲדוֹן עוֹלָם אֲשֶׁר מָלַךְ,   בְּטֶרֶם כָּל יְצִיר נִבְרָא.

לְעֵת נַעֲשָׂה בְחֶפְצוֹ כֹּל,   אֲזַי מֶלֶךְ שְׁמוֹ נִקְרָא.

וְאַחֲרֵי כִּכְלוֹת הַכֹּל,   לְבַדּוֹ יִמְלֹךְ נוֹרָא.

וְהוּא הָיָה וְהוּא הֹוֶה,   וְהוּא יִהְיֶה בְּתִפְאָרָה.

וְהוּא אֶחָד וְאֵין שֵׁנִי,   לְהַמְשִׁיל לוֹ לְהַחְבִּירָה.

בְּלִי רֵאשִׁית בְּלִי תַכְלִית,   וְלוֹ הָעֹז וְהַמִּשְׂרָה.

וְהוּא אֵלִי וְחַי גֹּאֲלִי,   וְצוּר חֶבְלִי בְּעֵת צָרָה.

וְהוּא נִסִּי וּמָנוֹס לִי,   מְנָת כּוֹסִי בְּיוֹם אֶקְרָא.

בְּיָדוֹ אַפְקִיד רוּחִי,   בְּעֵת אִישַׁן וְאָעִירָה.

וְעִם רוּחִי גְּוִיָּתִי,   יהוה לִי וְלֹא אִירָא.

body and soul. One should always strive to support himself by his own labor rather than live on charity (Radak).

אַשְׁרֶיךָ — *You are fortunate* — in this world; וְטוֹב לָךְ, *and it is well with you* — in the Hereafter (*Avos* 4:1).

Similarly, *Midrash Tanchuma* cautions that one should not rely on miracles or זְכוּת אָבוֹת, *ancestral merit.* Only after one exerts his own efforts at spiritual improvement does God send His blessing.

בְּיַרְכְּתֵי בֵיתֶךָ — *In the inner chambers of your home.* I.e., modestly reserving herself for her husband (*Tanchuma*).

שְׁתִלֵי זֵיתִים — *Olive shoots.* The olive, unlike other shoots, cannot be grafted (*Rashi*). [This metaphorically describes Israel's determination not to intermarry with the nations.]

סָבִיב לְשֻׁלְחָנֶךָ — *Surrounding your table.* The entire family together under your own loving care (*R' Hirsch*).

וּרְאֵה בְּטוּב יְרוּשָׁלָיִם — *And may you gaze upon the good of Jerusalem.* May you be redeemed from exile, *and gaze upon the good of Jerusalem* as you return to the Holy City (*Radak*).

וּרְאֵה בָנִים לְבָנֶיךָ — *And may you see children born to your children.* A blessing of longevity; may you enjoy the company of grandchildren (*Radak*).

שָׁלוֹם עַל יִשְׂרָאֵל — *Peace upon Israel!* "The Holy One, Blessed is He, found no vessel that could contain blessing for Israel except that of peace" (last Mishnah in *Uktzin*).

◆§ רִגְזוּ וְאַל תֶּחֱטָאוּ / **Tremble and sin not** [*Psalms* 4:5].

Tremble [in awe and fear] before the Holy One, Blessed is He, and do not sin (*Rashi*).

Homiletically, this verse exhorts Israel to tremble so much at the thought of sin that the very idea of transgression becomes disturbing and traumatic. The phrase would mean: '*be distressed and upset*' by the prospect of sin. Furthermore, be distressed over your previous sins and thus you will not sin again (*Shaarei Teshuvah* 1:4).[1]

1. The Talmud (*Berachos* 5a) interprets this verse homiletically. 'A person should constantly provoke his יֵצֶר טוֹב, *good inclination*, to battle against his יֵצֶר הָרָע, *evil inclination*, as it says, רִגְזוּ וְאַל תֶּחֱטָאוּ, literally, *provoke* or *agitate and do not sin*. If he succeeds in defeating the evil inclination, all is well. If

fruitful vine in the inner chambers of your home,° your children like olive shoots° surrounding your table.° Behold! — so shall be blessed the man who fears God. May HASHEM bless you from Zion and may you gaze upon the good of Jerusalem° all the days of your life. And may you see children born to your children,° peace upon Israel!°

Psalms 4:5

Tremble and sin not.° Reflect in your hearts while on your beds, and be utterly silent. Selah.

Siddur Shacharis

Master of the universe,° Who reigned
before any form was created,
At the time when His will brought all into being —
then His Name was proclaimed as King.°
After all has ceased to be,°
He, the Awesome one, will reign alone.
It is He Who was, He Who is,
and He Who shall remain, in splendor.
He is One — there is no second
to compare to Him to declare as His equal.
Without beginning° and with no end° —
He is the power and dominion.
He is my God, my living Redeemer,
Rock of my pain in time of distress.
He is my banner, and refuge° for me,
the portion in my cup on the day I call.
Into His hand I shall entrust my spirit
when I go to sleep — and I shall awaken!°
With my spirit shall my body remain,°
HASHEM is with me, I shall not fear.

אֲדוֹן עוֹלָם — **Adon Olam.**
This beautiful *zemer* has been attributed to R' Shlomo ibn Gabirol, one of the greatest early *paytanim*. It praises God as the King, Creator, Infinite, and All-Powerful. It is especially appropriate for the night because of its closing stanzas: "Into His hand I shall entrust my spirit when I go to sleep ..."
The following commentary has been selected from the ArtScroll *Siddur* by Rabbi Nosson Scherman.

אֲזַי מֶלֶךְ שְׁמוֹ נִקְרָא — *Then His Name was*

proclaimed as King. Although God was Master and reigned before anything existed, there were, as yet, no beings who could proclaim His majesty. Only when He desired to bring *everything into being* could His title of 'King' be proclaimed (ibid.).

וְאַחֲרֵי כִּכְלוֹת הַכֹּל — *After all has ceased to be.* The universe will not be destroyed, because God promised that Israel is His eternal nation. But *wickedness* will cease to be. As long as the wicked hold sway, they prevent universal acknowledgment of His

not, he should engage in Torah study, as it says, אִמְרוּ בִלְבַבְכֶם, *'reflect in your hearts.'* If he is victorious, all is well. If not, he should recite the portion of *Shema* [through which one accepts the yoke of God's sovereignty] when he lies down to sleep, as it says, עַל מִשְׁכַּבְכֶם, *'while on your beds.'* If he conquers, all is well. If not, he should remind himself of the awesome day of death, as it says, וְדֹמּוּ סֶלָה, *'and be utterly silent, selah.'*
The Sages vividly emphasize that life is a constant struggle to curb our base lusts and desires. *Chovos haLevavos (Yichud haMa'aseh, 5)* records that a pious man once encountered a band of soldiers coming home from battle. He said to them: 'The war from which you return was only a relatively minor skirmish. Prepare yourselves now for normal, daily living which is a truly great war against the evil inclination and his agents' (see *Overview* to ArtScroll *Tehillim*).

sovereignty. With them gone, *He will reign alone,* in the sense that none will doubt Him *(Etz Yosef).*

בְּלִי רֵאשִׁית — *Without beginning.* God is not a physical being and is totally independent. He is unbounded by time or space *(Etz Yosef).*

בְּלִי תַכְלִית — *And with no end.* Since He exists forever, by definition, God can have infinite patience. Unlike a human king who may feel constrained to carry out his policies while he still has the energy and dominion to do so, God knows that His plan can proceed unhurried and uninterrupted. This strengthens our faith immeasurably, for we know that His promises and purposes will be fulfilled, even though that may take many human lifetimes *(ibid.).*

נִסִּי וּמָנוֹס — *My banner, and refuge.* In triumph He is the *banner* that guides me, *(R' Hirsch);* in defeat He is my protecting *refuge (Etz Yosef).*

וְאָעִירָה — *And I shall awaken!* [Though I deposit my spirit into God's safekeeping every night when I go to sleep, I do so with confidence that He will restore it to me in the morning, *I shall awaken!* — refreshed and ready for a new day of accomplishment.]

וְעִם רוּחִי גְוִיָּתִי — *With my spirit shall my body remain.* I know that God will reunite my body and my spirit, so I have no fear *(Etz Yosef).*

תם ונשלם שבח לאל בורא עולם

Meir Zlotowitz
Rosh Chodesh Shevat, 5742 / January, 1982
Brooklyn, New York

◆§ Shema and the Ten Commandments

The Talmud *(Tamid* 32a) relates that the Ten Commandments were recited in the Temple as part of *Shema* liturgy, because, like the *Shema*, they are a basic declaration of the Jewish faith. The Sages once considered following this practice as part of the regular daily service, but the proposal was withdrawn because of the מִינִים, *heretics*, who would have maliciously cited the practice as proof that only the Ten Commandments were given by God at Sinai but not the rest of the Torah *(Berachos* 12a). Nevertheless, *Yerushalmi (Berachos* 1:5) demonstrates how each of the Ten Commandments is alluded to in the words of the *Shema* itself:

☐ *I am HASHEM your God* is echoed in שְׁמַע יִשְׂרָאֵל ה' אֱלֹהֵינוּ — *Hear O Israel, HASHEM is our God;*

☐ *You shall not recognize the gods of others* is paralleled by ה' אֶחָד, *HASHEM is One* — the only One;

☐ *You shall not take the Name of HASHEM your God in a vain oath* coincides with וְאָהַבְתָּ אֵת ה' אֱלֹהֶיךָ, *You shall love HASHEM, your God* — for one who truly loves his king will not swear falsely in his name;

☐ *Remember the Sabbath day* is alluded to in לְמַעַן תִּזְכְּרוּ, *so that you shall remember and do all My mitzvos* — for Scripture equates Sabbath observance with the fulfillment of the totality of all *mitzvos; 'Your holy Sabbath did You make known to them, and mitzvos, decrees and Torah did You command them'* (Nehemiah 9:14).

☐ *Honor your father and mother so that you may live a long life* is found in לְמַעַן יִרְבּוּ, *that your days and the days of your children may be increased.*

☐ *You shall not kill,* if transgressed, will be punished by וַאֲבַדְתֶּם מְהֵרָה, *you will be swiftly destroyed* — for he who kills shall be killed.

☐ *You shall not commit adultery* can be adhered to only if you obey לֹא תָתוּרוּ, *you shall not be led astray after your heart and eyes* — for these organs are the agents *provocateur* of sin [the eyes see and the heart desires];

☐ *You shall not steal from another* is reflected in וְאָסַפְתָּ דְגָנֶךָ, *you will gather 'your' wheat,* — your own wheat and not your neighbor's;

☐ *You shall not bear false witnesss,* rather you shall follow in the paths of ה' אֱלֹהֵיכֶם אֱמֶת, *HASHEM, your God, Who is truth;* and

☐ *You shall not covet your neighbor's house* is implied in the *mitzvah* of *mezuzah,* which is on the doorpost of 'your' house, — your own house, not your neighbor's.

Thus, whoever recites the *Shema* is, in effect, affirming the Ten Commandments as well (ArtScroll *Aseres HaDibros/*Ten Commandments, by Rabbi Avrohom Chaim Feuer, pp. 63-64).

This volume is part of
THE ARTSCROLL SERIES®
an ongoing project of
translations, commentaries and expositions
on Scripture, Mishnah, Talmud, Halachah,
liturgy, history, the classic Rabbinic writings,
biographies and thought.

For a brochure of current publications
visit your local Hebrew bookseller
or contact the publisher:

Mesorah Publications, ltd.
4401 Second Avenue
Brooklyn, New York 11232
(718) 921-9000
www.artscroll.com